# Sweetly Sings Delaney

John Harding

GREENWICH EXCHANGE
LONDON

**Greenwich Exchange, London**

Sweetly Sings Delaney
©John Harding 2014

First published in Great Britain in 2014
All rights reserved

Printed and bound by **imprint**digital.net
Typesetting and layout by Jude Keen Limited, London
Tel: 020 8355 4541
Cover design by December Publications, Belfast
Tel: 028 90286559
Cover picture: ©2013 Getty Images
Back cover picture: Courtesy of Harold Riley

Greenwich Exchange Website: www.greenex.co.uk

Cataloguing in Publication Data is available
from the British Library.

ISBN: 978-1-906075-83-5

Most of us know what we want but how many of us recognise it when we get it? We can't choose the time and the place into which we are born – maybe a restless city alive and dying in the same breath – and it can mean many different things to many different people but more often than not it can be like a terrible drug – you really want to get away from it and give it up but you can't. So you stay. Maybe reach a compromise with it or perhaps you fight a pitched battle with it all the days of your life.

Shelagh Delaney,
Prologue in programme for *The Lion in Love*, September 1960

I write as people talk.

Shelagh Delaney, *The Times*, 2nd February 1959

# Contents

Photo: Courtesy of Murray Melvin

Shelagh Delaney chats to (from left) Nigel Davenport, Clifton Jones and Murray Melvin in the dressing room backstage at Wyndham's Theatre, February 1959.

# Foreword

*"I would love a cup, our Murray, if there's one going."*

This in reply to an offer of tea on our first meeting, introduced by Joan Littlewood, in the foyer of the Theatre Royal, Stratford East.

I was always *"our Murray"*.

The impact of that voice and the person was enormous and was to grow as she matured. Here was a nineteen-year-old who sounded and looked voluptuous. She would have liked that compliment. She liked the rhythm and cadence of words.

None of us was aware at that tea-making moment that she would, with the working methods of Joan and the Theatre Workshop Company, help change the attitudes and practices of English theatre.

I am delighted that John Harding has given us the opportunity to glimpse some insights to her journey that was indeed extraordinary.

**Murray Melvin**

# Preface

When Shelagh Delaney died in November 2011, fulsome tributes were paid to her in newspapers and magazines from all over the world. The obituaries emphasised the important contribution she had made to the theatre with her seminal play, *A Taste of Honey*, and all paid tribute to its impact on so many different levels. There was a tendency, however, to underplay the rest of her literary output, to suggest that after *Honey* she failed to match up to the promise she had shown as an *ingénue* writer.

This small book seeks to demonstrate that Shelagh Delaney, in fact, played an important role in both stage and film writing in the decade that followed her initial success, and that her contribution to the careers of film directors such as Lindsay Anderson and Tony Richardson was a significant one. It also looks closely at her relationship with her home city of Salford, particularly in the light of the harsh criticism she endured from certain quarters of Salford society from the very outset of her career.

I'd like to thank Anne McGuire, Barbara D. Goldstone and Ida Bede for their memories of Shelagh as a young girl and, in particular, Bill Gray (and sister Shirley Evans) for memories of Shelagh in Salford and for help in general with the period.

I would like to thank Duncan McCormick at Salford Local History Library and Gillian Spark at Rose Bruford College for help with research; Professor Phil Tew for literary guidance; and Janet Unwin for textual corrections and editorial help. Thank you, once again, to Henry Maas for his close attention to detail.

A special thank you must go to Harold Riley for his invaluable help with early memories of Shelagh and also for allowing us to use his excellent photographs of Salford's Brindle Heath district.

Finally, thank you to Murray Melvin for writing the Foreword, which serves as both a personal memory of and a tribute to Shelagh.

# 1

# Salford

My father worked hard and he spent hard. We had a darn good time in Salford.

Shelagh Delaney, *Daily Mail*, February 1959

Shelagh Delaney was born on 25th November 1938 in the Hope Hospital on Eccles Old Road, Salford, Lancashire. She was the first child of Joseph and Elsie Delaney née Twemlow. The family then lived at 67, New Thomas Street, Pendleton, a street that still exists but without any houses.

When she was born her father worked as a bus conductor ("Bus ticket numbers reckon up fortunes," she would write in her semi-autobiography).[1] On her birth certificate her name is spelled Sheila and it remained that way all through her school years. When and why she changed its spelling isn't known. In 1958, Brendan Behan, the Irish playwright and later a good friend, was moved to write to theatre director Joan Littlewood, "Why does she spell her name that way?" One can assume it was to move herself a little closer to her Irish roots, of which she was especially proud. "My grandparents were Irish," she would tell reporters when she first came to prominence, "and my father was half-Irish."[2]

The city of Salford into which she was born was, in the late 1930s, one of the most deprived in Britain. Karl Marx's great collaborator Friedrich Engels famously lived and worked there in the mid-19th century and his observations of working-class conditions, especially the Irish immigrants living in slum housing, were unequivocal:

The working people live, almost all of them, in wretched, damp, filthy cottages … the streets which surround them are usually in the most miserable and filthy condition, laid out without the slightest reference to ventilation, with reference solely to the profit secured by the contractor …'[3]

Things had changed little for working people in the years between the publication of Engels' *Condition of the Working Class in England* in 1844 and Shelagh's appearance on the scene in 1938. A National Rat Week commenced in the very same week of her birth, the local *Salford City Reporter* newspaper announcing: 'War Declared on the Vermin'. The paper revealed that in the past years two rat-catchers had paid 7,700 visits to various premises and caught 2,261 live rats. Thousands more had been destroyed.[4]

Salford excelled in such negative statistics. The city's infantile death rate at the time was 90 per thousand, exceeding all British cities other than Newcastle. Its maternal mortality figure was also exceeded only by neighbouring Manchester and by Newcastle, but was rising: in 1936 it was 4.34; in 1938: 5.7.[5]

In July 1938, according to an official children's health report, of 9,500 children inspected between the ages of five and twelve, 898 suffered from throat or nose disease, 674 from defective vision and 125 from lung disease. More than 5,000 had inflamed or septic gums. In another report, eczema, impetigo and sores were found in 3,332 out of 6,519 children examined.

Much of the ill health was caused by the city's deadly atmosphere. Comparing Salford to South Kensington's sunshine revealed that Salford's daily mean solar radiation was as low as 3.3 in December and 5.26 in February compared to 23.8 and 35.5 respectively in that favoured district of London. Whenever it rained, in one particular district of the Salford there arose, "an unpleasant acetous odour" said to derive from deposits of calcium acetate used in calico (cotton) printing found in the soil between the pavements.[6]

Twenty years later and the situation was hardly any better. In mid-1959 a Parliamentary question from Salford East's Labour MP Frank Allaun concerning pollution in the city revealed that it was twice as bad as in Manchester, with sulphur dioxide heavier in the ratio of 14 to 11. Bronchitis death rates were twice the national average, with 1,200 chronic cases in the city, while Salford's 'standardised mortality rate' (calculated against national average) for stomach cancer was the highest in Britain. "These figures", Allaun said, "mean that three people out of every five who die from these diseases would not have done so had Salford's air been reasonably smoke-free."[7]

Scarred, stained and polluted by the industrial revolution, Salford had by then been immortalised in song by the singer and dramatist Ewan MacColl and in paint by the artist L.S. Lowry. Both would have an influence on Delaney's work.

MacColl, born and raised in harsh conditions in the Broughton district of the city close to where Shelagh would also grow up, explained towards the end of his life: "My relationship with Salford has been a love-hate one … I can't bear the place. At the same time, everything I do, everything I've ever written, is to some extent informed by my experiences in Salford."[8]

The tensions that MacColl identifies between pride and shame, powerful identification and disavowal, firmly rooted identity and desire for the freedom of flight and self-reinvention, are recurrent motifs that would also characterise Delaney's creative relationship with the city. Like Shelagh, MacColl was one to whom ethnic roots were crucial. The son of expatriate Scottish parents, he was originally called Jimmie Miller but, once established in London, he changed his name to reflect his sympathies with the Lallans movement in Scotland which sought to integrate, blend and combine various forms of the Scots language, both vernacular and archaic.

In fact, MacColl would come to play a crucial, if indirect, part in Delaney's working life. 'Dirty Old Town' was originally composed by him to cover a scene change in MacColl's Salford-set 1949 play *Landscape with Chimneys*. It was one of many short radical plays written for the Theatre Union, later to become the Theatre Workshop, a company MacColl and his wife, Joan Littlewood, had created in Manchester, which would eventually settle in East London. It would be with Theatre Workshop that Shelagh would find early and enduring fame.

'Dirty Old Town' is about a young man courting a girl in grimy, polluted Salford. With its references to smells and smoke, to cats prowling and ships' sirens calling, it's an early piece of poetic realism prefiguring in certain crucial respects Delaney's first major play. And, just as with Delaney's work, MacColl's song would prove to be too real for the afflicted but proud city of Salford. A still religious-minded city (the annual religious Whit (Whitsuntide) Walks were a greatly anticipated event), jealously protective of its customs, fearful of its encroaching neighbour Manchester, resentful of the South and the latter's perceived condescension, 'conservative' in nature despite the Labour Party's dominance in local politics, Salford was not, in the second half of the twentieth century, a place at ease with itself. MacColl's work featured regularly on radio in the 1940s and 1950s and when he first wrote 'Dirty Old Town', the local council were unhappy at having Salford depicted in such a negative way. After considerable criticism, one phrase in the lyrics was changed: from "smelled the smoke on the Salford wind" to "smelled the spring on the smoky wind".

Lowry's relationship to the city where he grew up and which he documented was less complicated than MacColl's. In 1963, revisiting come of the Salford scenes he'd painted, he remarked that little had changed and that he'd "always hated the place".

Nevertheless, his depictions of the North, of the city of Salford in particular, were by the 1950s becoming as ubiquitous as to seem, as one critic noted, "indistinguishable from the reality ... accepted as the Authorised Version of life in the north".[9]

It was an industrial Lancashire that had been highly sanitised, a world in which, as Mervyn Levy put it, grime and squalor had become "something very clean and pure, even poetic".[10] Lowry was seen as the artist who had discovered "beauty" amidst the grime of industrial Britain, who had made the North an object of aesthetic veneration. This would be an important element in the reception of Shelagh's work, particularly on film, as we shall see.

She herself became aware of Lowry's work very early on in life. She wrote in 1961: "Every school in Salford has to its credit a Lowry painting – whether it is an original on loan from the art gallery or a reproduction – and every child in the city grew up as I grew up with this artist's vision of their own particular world before them. *Coming from the mill* was the first of Lowry's paintings that I saw and I remember that it used to hang on our classroom wall just left of the blackboard and the teacher's desk and when attention wandered from lessons – which was often enough – it usually found its way over to the Mill picture and stayed there."[11]

What is interesting about her assessment of his paintings, however, is not that she recognised the industrial scenes that surrounded her as she grew up, nor that she felt they were beautiful. Instead, she grasped something more essential about his work: Lowry's depiction of people. As a child, she spotted something that for many decades art critics missed entirely. "In L.S. Lowry is the very essence of a child, and any child coming face to face with his work will recognise instinctively what it is all about. Crowds crowds crowds. A child knows just how lonely a crowd can be. The crowd coming from the mill, the crowd gathering together at the scene of an accident, the crowd passing through the streets in the shadow of a black high-steepled Northern church – the crowd – always related to their surroundings – never ever related to each other. The universal truth – this solitariness of mankind – this loneliness is something or other we have always suspected at some time and Lowry has caught it – comic, cruel, beautiful, ugly and tragic."[12]

Back in Salford in late 1938, however, as Shelagh was being taken home from Hope Hospital, preparations were afoot to cope with more potent threats than rats and pollution-related diseases. With a war looming large on the horizon, evacuation plans were being drawn up in the city: 200,000 respirators were being issued to schools and air-raid trenches were being planned within the city to accommodate 200,000.

Air attacks on Manchester began on 8th August 1940, when German bombers dropped several high explosive bombs along with incendiaries. The raids became heavier later that month and into September: no area of the city would escape damage. Four years after Shelagh's birth at Hope Hospital, fourteen nurses would die there in what later became known as the Salford blitz.

Thus, her early childhood would be dominated by wartime restrictions and privations; the conflict would bring disruption and dislocation for the Delaney family. On its outbreak, Joe Delaney joined the 2nd Battalion of the XXth Lancashire Fusiliers. He was subsequently wounded and returned home in 1943. An avid reader and storyteller, he would recount his experiences in North Africa to Shelagh, an equally keen listener. Shelagh told a *Times* reporter: "… true stories about his war experiences in the Lancashire Fusiliers – North Africa. Monte Cassino. He was badly wounded at Medjez el Bab and two Germans helped him. An officer handed his gun over to them and they let him be taken back to hospital. They said something which meant, 'War is no good.' He used to tell me it in German, but I can't remember the words."[13]

Throughout the war years, the Delaneys would move frequently. Shelagh later wrote: "Many a time I imagine some of the noises I know and see things and remember things of sirens and searchlights, gasmask and shelter, ours and theirs going over, all-clear. Back to bed again. Street parties and flags out flying for victory. All smiles."[14]

The smiles were short-lived. The disruption and upheaval along with the trying conditions of existence in post-war Salford would adversely affect her health. Aged 11, she was sent to a children's convalescent home in Lytham St Annes, a common experience for children from deprived areas whose physical state had been blighted by poor diet and unhealthy housing. Fresh air and good food plus regular medical supervision were considered essential to overcoming the effects of diseases such as rickets and diphtheria.

Her stay at the home would form the basis of her first major piece of prose, the semi-autobiographical prose work, 'Sweetly Sings the Donkey', published in the eponymous volume of collected writings in 1962. Her scattered recollections, recounted through reconstructed conversations, dramatic situations and stream-of-consciousness passages, give us a glimpse into a distant and now forgotten world, but one of crucial importance to her as a writer.

It's a world populated by characters such as the neighbour who liked to visit corpses laid out in other people's houses: "When I was little I used to think it was a good luck token to see a dead body, like touching a sailor's collar or seeing a pin and picking it up, but as I got older I realized it was a hobby, always received reservedly in our house." The woman, she recalled, would visit the Delaney household and chatter about her most recent viewing: "'Candles all round the coffin. Her cheeks were so rosy and her lips were so red.' And my father would wink at me and my mother would spit on the iron. The spit hissed at the iron's heat and bounced off it like lead shot."[15]

It was a world where grandmothers pawned their wedding rings; where people who saw a nun approaching unfastened their coats and kept them unfastened until they saw a four-footed animal ("something to do with letting the Holy Ghost in", Shelagh commented); where the cure for whooping cough was to eat a fried mouse, "fried in butter"; a world of de-mob suits and ex-soldiers suffering from shell-shock.

The convalescent home in which she was placed was run by an order of strict and censorious Catholic nuns – perfect subjects for a girl with a mind of her own, a keenly observant eye and a sly, rebellious streak in her nature. She herself was privileged, sleeping in a private room at the top of the house with a view of the sea ("The windows are iron-barred like in looney-bins …") but, like any child, she was unhappy to be so far from home.

"These and all sorts of other things I remember but why I remember I don't know. Sometimes I think it is because I am frightened being here in this place and miles away from home but when I try to find a cause of being frightened I can't and begin to think it is not fear I feel at all but something else."[16]

The home was, first and foremost, a place for regaining one's health, although Shelagh remained sceptical: viewing her fellow inmates she mused: "Some of them have been here for years and they don't look any healthier than I do now, so if this convalescent place does me as much good as it seems to have done them, it's hopeless and I've had it."

She was particularly scathing about the food: "For tea today we had bread and blackcurrant jam – washed down with a cup of cocoa. It was very good but at home it would only be considered a fill-in for between proper meals. I would sooner have the sort of teas we have at home and could just eat a plate of potato pie, gravy, red cabbage and apple crumble and custard."[17]

She noted: "Every morning we are carefully weighed and measured. I am the tallest, thinnest girl in the place and they are trying to build me up by stuffing me with iron pills, brown malt cod-liver oil, and bottles of Scott's Emulsion with so many vitamins piling up inside me I'm bound to explode sooner or later into a big mushroom cloud."[18]

There was the ubiquitous sun-ray treatment administered to millions of children in the decades immediately following the Second World War; there were also long walks by the seashore and extended periods of enforced rest.

The nuns, inevitably, found it difficult to deal with Shelagh, given her quick wit and sharp tongue exacerbated by the all-prevailing boredom. When she asks permission to read a book, ("The books are in prison just like me") she is told to read the Bible but retorts that she's already read it. She asks whether, instead of sewing, she could write or read and she is refused permission.

> I decided to go on strike and put my tools down.
> "What are you doing?" the nun inquired.
> "Thinking."
> "What about?"
> "The Sufferings of St John of the Cross."[19]

Her observations of her fellow 'inmates' reveal her as somewhat mature beyond her years, a characteristic that would cause concern years later when her first play was produced. Commenting on how another girl, when sent precious toffee coupons from home, is forced by the nuns to hand out the sweets to the others, she records that the girl is horrified at having to share them out and that the girls who receive them are uncomfortable about getting them. "Left alone, she'd have probably given them out of her own free will and everyone would have been happier."[20]

She's also alive to the secrets other girls are ignorant of. One girl had been in various children's homes "because of something her father did to her. The something is incest. When you ask the chief gossipers what incest is they think quickly and say: 'Oh, it's extreme cruelty. He burnt her with cigarette ends and beat her with a poker.' Only Nina and myself and

Kitty Skidmore know what incest really is. If we told the other girls they'd faint …"[21]

It is in the story 'Sweetly Sings the Donkey' that Delaney first reveals something of her junior school days. Interviewed by a snobbish government inspector, she is asked what sort of school she attended. When she says a state school the inspector says "Good". Shelagh asks what's good about it and is told that girls 'of her class' would never have received an education many years before: "You are a fortunate child indeed to have been born into a compassionate and enlightened age." That she has failed her entrance exam for high school was also, according to the inspector, a blessing. "At secondary school you will be receiving an education suited to your capabilities."

In fact, Delaney's subsequent education would become something of a contentious issue in the early years of her rise to literary fame. She was keen to present herself as a non-achiever and delighted in painting a picture of herself as someone doomed to failure. In *Sweetly*, she summarises her (fictional?) junior school reports:

> Has worked hard this term. Does not exert herself sufficiently. Unwilling to accept discipline. Has some originality of thought. A likeable girl. Inclined to sullenness. Uncommunicative. Over-imaginative. Has difficulty distinguishing fact from fiction. This girl is a liar. Expect improvement next term. Position in class examination – ninth. Number of children in class – fifty-two. Times absent – ten. Times late -forty-three. This will not do.[22]

In 1960, talking to camera in Ken Russell's BBC *Monitor* programme she summarised her secondary schooldays thus:

> I went to school, I went to about five different schools between the age of five and nine and I didn't pass the eleven plus or anything, I went to a Secondary Modern school, and I was there till I was fifteen, which was marvellous because … the best education I ever had, was when I was at that school, and then when I was fifteen, for some reason, I don't know … perhaps it was because I was a bit more cheeky than the rest, a bit more conspicuous, I was moved to a grammar school, and when I got there I thought, oh, you know, crikey, I'll be very much behind the door, as far as knowing things is concerned, I had a shock, actually, because I realised that so far as knowing anything was concerned that I knew a damn sight more than a lot of the girls there did and this to me was the sad thing because I knew that, back at the Secondary school that I'd been

sent from, half the girls and half the boys were just as capable at doing, the same sort of things as I was doing and knowing as much as I knew and it seemed a terrible shame to me that they should be left there with the prospect of leaving school at fifteen …[23]

Interviewed a year earlier for *The Times* by Laurence Kitchin, she said: "I was at three different primary schools – confusing? No, I enjoyed the change. My father rang them up after I took the 11-plus but they said there were not enough places in the high school."[24]

In fact, she had been transferred from Broughton Secondary School to nearby Pendleton Grammar school because, according to her Mathematics teacher, Miss A.C. Davies, although she could do no arithmetic and hadn't passed her eleven-plus exam, "… there was something so special about her that Salford Education Committee made a very special exception in her case."[25]

At 13 she was the 'Librarian' of the secondary school's History Club that met on Wednesdays after school. The club invited speakers: a policewoman, a JP; it held talks and mounted a 'Brains Trust'. The members visited local places of interest, the oldest church in Salford (Holy Trinity) and Heaton Hall, and pursued a 'learn by looking' exercise: "We try to imagine how people lived at different times, pictures and models of their clothes …" There were also visits to London.

In the July 1952 issue of the school magazine there appeared a small character sketch by Shelagh entitled 'The Vagabond':

> His battered, torn cap was pushed back on a curly crop of hair that needed cutting and combing. Tweed should have been the cloth of his jacket, but now, oh! It looked like a coconut matting of various unearthly colours … He wore the remains of a shirt that looked grey but, I think, must have entered the world as a crisp, clean white …

Once at Pendleton she continued to excel. The history mistress Constance Cummings recalled in 1959: "You could always talk to Shelagh as a grown-up. She was very mature even when she came to us. She was quick to de-bunk the other girls' awful silliness about boyfriends and make-up – with a chuckle."[26]

She was a deputy librarian at the school and was recalled by fellow pupil Anne McGuire as, "a natural leader and she soon had a coterie of friends. She was made form captain during my final year. One of many memories was her playing 'ragtime jazz' on the grand piano in the main hall of the school, which was against the rules many of which Sheila quite often broke, being such a free spirit. I was forever grateful to her when she helped a group of bullies get expelled after they made mine and others' lives a misery ..."

That she was also a budding writer is evident from another recollection, this time of a family friend, Shirley Evans:

> She used to come to our house with another young girl friend of mine and she always had a pad and pencil with her. My dad used to tell us to be careful what we said when she was with us because he was sure she was taking notes. She didn't do much note-taking but she did do a lot of laughing because that was the kind of household we were.[27]

NOTES
1  *Sweetly Sings the Donkey* (SSD) (Penguin, 1968), p. 37.
2  *The Times*, 2nd February 1959.
3  *The Condition of the Working-Class in England in 1844*, trans. Florence K. Wischnewetzky (Cosimo, 2009), p. 63.
4  *Salford City Reporter* (*SCR*), 21st October 1938.
5  *SCR*, 1st July 1938.
6  *SCR*, 15th July 1938.
7  *SCR*, 16th February 1959.
8  Ben Harker, *Class Act: The Cultural and Political Life of Ewan MacColl* (Pluto Press, 2007), p. 5.
9  Chris Waters, 'Representations of Everyday Life: L.S. Lowry and the Landscape of Memory in Postwar Britain', *Representations*, 65 (Winter 1999), pp. 121–40.
10  Ibid.
11  Shelagh Delaney, 'L.S. Lowry', *Studio*, 162, 821 (September 1961).
12  Ibid.
13  *The Times*, 2nd February 1959.
14  *SSD*, p. 36.
15  *SSD*, p. 81.
16  *SSD*, p. 38.
17  *SSD*, p. 16.
18  *SSD*, p. 12.
19  *SSD*, p. 14.
20  *SSD*, p. 15.
21  *SSD*, p. 39.
22  *SSD*, p. 37.
23  *Shelagh Delaney's Salford*, BBC, *Monitor*, 25th September 1960.
24  *Times*, 2nd February 1959.
25  *Daily Sketch*, 12thFebruary 1959.
26  Ibid.
27  Letter to author from Shirley Evans, 2013.

Shelagh Delaney (right) in Hartington Street, Salford, aged 8, with friend Jackie Shaw.

# 2

# A Little Epic

When I was seventeen I was in a terrible mess ... I knew
I wanted to do something but what? ... I was lucky,
I thought I could write, I had that to deal with and I was
lucky, I was dead lucky ...

Shelagh Delaney, BBC *Monitor*,
September 1960

In early 1958 at the age of nineteen Shelagh sent a copy of her first play,
*A Taste of Honey*, to Joan Littlewood at the Theatre Workshop in London.
Along with it she enclosed the following letter:

Dear Miss Littlewood,

Along with this letter comes a play, the first I have written. I wondered if
you would read it through and send it back to me because no matter what
sort of theatrical atrocity it might be, it isn't valueless so far as I'm
concerned. A fortnight ago I didn't know the theatre existed, but a young
man, anxious to improve my mind, took me to the Opera House in
Manchester and I came away after the performance having suddenly
realised that at last, after nineteen years of life, I had discovered something
that meant more to me than myself. I sat down and thought. The
following day I bought a packet of paper and borrowed an unbelievable
typewriter which I still have great difficulty in using. I set to and produced
this little epic – don't ask me why – I'm quite unqualified for anything
like this. But at least I finished it and if, from among the markings and the
typing errors and the spelling mistakes, you can gather a little sense from
what I have written – or a little nonsense – I should be extremely grateful
for your criticism – though I hate criticism of any kind.

I want to write for the theatre, but I know so very little about it. I know nothing, have nothing – except a willingness to learn – and intelligence.
Yours sincerely,
Shelagh Delaney [1]

The letter is interesting as it sowed the seeds of many a myth concerning her rapid progress from anonymous teenager to international literary celebrity. It also reveals her as someone with a forthright attitude and not a little confidence despite the declaration of ignorance.

Delaney would give few clues away as to her life prior to the writing of *A Taste of Honey*. As we have seen, of her time at grammar school she was casually dismissive, preferring to laud her secondary school as having been more useful to her even though she obtained five GCE passes at Pendleton. She left school, however, before attempting further education. She told Robert Muller: "No, I'm not an intellectual myself. I'm more intelligent than intellectual, if you know what I mean. I don't regret not having had a university education. I realised it wasn't suitable for me. I haven't got the discipline to turn myself into a scholar somehow. I wouldn't have got in, anyway. I only had a couple of years of grammar school."[2]

She clearly had no intention of taking the traditional professional route for an intelligent young woman of the time, that of teaching. Of her post-school days and subsequentl employment she elaborated just a little when penning an author's biography for her American publisher:

> Saturday morning job in milk factory counting bottles. Asked to retire from position gracefully owing to inability to count correctly. On leaving school found job in gown shop – left voluntarily after one week's service. Worked as usherette in Manchester Opera House – sacked for fraternising with actors. Obtained employment in Research Lab. of Metropolitan-Vickers Electrical Co. Trafford Park, Salford. Lancashire. Worked for eighteen months as photographer's assistant until play *A Taste of Honey* was produced and made me rich and famous.[3]

The Vickers job was her longest: "There was a great variety of people to get to know. All the time I intended to write. I knew I could, by comparing my essays with the ones the other girls wrote at school."[4]

When asked by Robert Muller what she enjoyed doing as a teenager she was flippant once again: "Well, the usual sort of thing. Creating a disturbance, mainly. But I got fed up with all the jobs I had. The job I hated most was in a gown-shop in the off-season. Nobody ever came in.

It drove me up the wall. I liked being an usherette most, I think. It gave me a chance to observe the audience. It taught me a lot about what kind of people go to the theatre. A lot of them seemed to be sort of frustrated intellectuals."[5]

In the various interviews she gave immediately following the success of *A Taste of Honey* she appeared keen to give the impression that theatre-going hardly featured at all in her life. She preferred instead to talk about more simple, working-class pleasures: "There was a tradition of popular culture: the music-hall and the 'penny crush', a ritual Saturday cinema show. That is what it used to be called," she told Laurence Kitchin in *The Times.*

> It was the week's climax for us, too, and we had a roaring time. We used to take part in it, laugh and shout. I remember in the Kit Canon [Carson?] serial there were masked men, dressed in black. We used to sort of traipse round the streets singing their song. Of course, there was pantomime. The first I saw was Goldilocks and the Three Bears. It was a habit to go the Salford Hippodrome and the cinema, often three times a week.[6]

The most she would publicly concede with regard to anything cultural in her early days was an almost accidental exposure to Shakespeare.

> I'd been kept in after school at Broughton Secondary. I had done something. I was in the headmistress's study and had just finished writing some lines. Miss Leek said to me: "I'm going upstairs to watch a performance of Othello. Do you want to see it?" It was by some school amateur group. I said to myself: Anything for a laugh … But I enjoyed Othello. It made a great impression on me. I was 12 at the time. I already realized I could write and I am grateful to Miss Leek. What I wrote she understood and she didn't harp so much as others on rigid English.[7]

Despite her constant protestations of ignorance, however ("A fortnight ago I didn't know the theatre existed"), by the time she wrote *TOH* she was extremely knowledgeable about the theatre. As she had already admitted, she had worked in one as an usherette, and then there was the mysterious 'young man' she mentioned in her letter to Joan Littlewood.

He turns out to have been the artist Harold Riley, and his recollections suggest that going to the theatre was a regular event and that Shelagh was far from being the naïve *ingénue* she was keen to depict herself as.

Harold Riley was a Salford boy, born in 1934. He had first encountered Delaney when she attended a drama presentation at Salford Grammar School where he was a pupil and appearing in *Henry IV Part 1* – in the title role. Salford Grammar then had a vibrant drama schedule and Harold recalled performances of Chekhov, Shakespeare and Bernard Shaw. "Looking down from the stage, I recall seeing her in the front row. We met afterwards and got on well and she would come to see the plays put on at Salford Grammar as her own school didn't do plays in such profusion."[8]

The two of them, as part of what Riley termed 'the cinema generation', became regular attenders at the various local movie houses, and would also spend free time in the café in the local Buile Park where there was a jukebox. It was the theatre, however, that was their greatest love. The local amateur group, the Salford Players, mounted a prolific programme running throughout the year, while in neighbouring Manchester there was both the Theatre Royal as well as the vibrant Manchester Library Theatre, housing a renowned repertory company.

Riley was struck at the time by the extent of Delaney's knowledge of the history of the theatre. He recalled walking through Manchester one evening to the Theatre Royal and, as they passed the Gaiety Cinema on the corner of Peter Street and Mount Street, which had once been the Gaiety Theatre, Shelagh remarked that she wished she had been able to meet a previous owner called Miss Horniman who had taken a company to New York before the First World War and had brought Sybil Thorndike back. "It was something I had been unaware of, but which I later confirmed when meeting and drawing Dame Thorndike herself."[9]

He continued: "She told me all about how Miss Horniman had bought and refurbished the Gaiety where she maintained an excellent repertory company putting on more than 200 plays, many by the so-called Manchester School, some directed by Lewis Casson who married Sybil Thorndike. The theatre disbanded in the 1920s but it had been the catalyst for the repertory theatre movement … and I realised, listening to Shelagh that she didn't only have a knowledge of the theatre and its history – she was steeped in it."[10]

That Delaney was more than just an interested visitor to the Manchester Library is clear from a recollection of veteran BBC radio drama producer Alfred Bradley who, in 1962, mounted a BBC radio production of *A Taste of Honey*. Bradley wrote: "Shelagh Delaney had an early taste of theatre when she met David Scase, the director of the Library Theatre in the pioneering days in Manchester, and asked him how she should go about becoming a producer. There were no vacancies for students in the company but Scase encouraged her to come along and watch rehearsals so that she would at least get the feel of the theatre. This tall, unobtrusive observant girl made no mention of her wish to write and the company was surprised when subsequently it discovered she had written *A Taste of Honey*."[11]

While she kept her writing a secret from professionals such as Scase, she would show things she had written to Riley. She would sometimes come to his painting studio and write, enjoying the peace and seclusion. Riley remembered: "She was a private person, but she would show her work to me because it was controversial – she lived in a tough district and saw what went on around her. She liked to shock. She had strong ideas about what she wanted to see in the theatre. She used to object to plays where factory workers come cap in hand and call the boss 'Sir'. Usually North Country people are shown as gormless, but Sheila believed they were very alive and cynical."[12]

In fact, she revealed that it was in 1954 when she was just sixteen that she first thought of writing professionally. It so happens that 1954 was the year another young woman with whom Delaney would be constantly compared shot to international literary fame.

In that year nineteen-year-old Françoise Sagan penned a short first novel entitled *Bonjour Tristesse* concerning an amoral teenager who sets out to prevent her philandering, widowed father from marrying again. It was originally published in France, and an English translation reached No. 1 on the *New York Times* best-seller list in 1955. Translated into twenty languages, it sold 2 million copies and was made into a film in 1958 directed by Otto Preminger and starring Jean Seberg, David Niven and Deborah Kerr.

Sagan was a phenomenon, famous at the time for her precocious, wayward personality as much as for her writing. She was considered a notorious representative of the younger generation, a symbol of fashionable rebellion in post-war Europe. With her gamine face and a penchant for whisky, fast cars and unconventional sex, the writer François Mauriac described her as "a charming little monster". With the royalties from *Tristesse* and its literary successors she bought a mink coat for her mother and a Jaguar for herself. In 1957 she would suffer severe head trauma after a speeding accident involving her Aston Martin.

The parallels with Delaney are intriguing and not simply because Sagan changed her name when submitting her début novel. Looking back three decades later, Sagan said the furore concerning her first novel resulted partly from the relationship between the heroine, Cécile, and her boyfriend. "It was inconceivable", she wrote, "that a young girl of 17 or 18 should make love without being in love with a boy of her own age, and not be punished for it." Furthermore, she added, people couldn't accept that this girl "should know about her father's love affairs, discuss them with him, and thereby reach a kind of complicity with him on subjects that had until then been taboo between parents and children". Similar incomprehension and outrage would be caused by *A Taste of Honey* and its young heroine, Jo, whose precociousness, her relationship with her feckless mother and her relationship to the facts of life were also considered unnatural.

In fact, from the very moment Shelagh stepped off the train from Salford just before the Stratford East premiere of *A Taste of Honey* in May 1958, Françoise Sagan's was the first name mentioned to her by a *Daily Mail* reporter as her possible role model. It so happened that some months earlier, amidst huge publicity, a ballet called *Le Rendez-vous Manqué* devised by Sagan had opened in London. Shelagh responded with a studied indifference: "I don't know much about her. I haven't read any of her books. I saw a bit of that ballet on television. Didn't think much of it."[13]

However, Delaney was a great reader: she later told the same newspaper reporter that she read, "everything that was going. French writers I liked. The Goncourt Brothers. Zola."[14]

She also claimed, like Sagan, to have written her début success in two weeks. She revealed to the *Guardian* many years later: "I tend to be lazy and only work when I have a sort of challenge … I think slowly and write quickly. I've got a very slow one-track mind. It takes me years to think. But I write very quickly, I need a deadline. One half of me is a perfectionist; the other is a lazy good-for-nothing."[15]

Her switch from prose to drama she explained quite simply: "I began *A Taste of Honey* as a novel but I was too busy enjoying myself, going out dancing. I wasn't getting very far with the novel and I suddenly realized I could do a play better." She then added an anecdote that would become legendary. She had been to see Terence Rattigan's play *Variation on a Theme*. She had not been impressed.

> "It seemed a sort of parade ground for the star to traipse about in Mr Norman Hartnell's creations. The thing that did get me was this: I think Miss Margaret Leighton is a great actress and I felt she was wasting her time. I just went home and started work."
>
> "In the evenings?"
>
> "No," said Miss Delaney obstinately as if still under the scrutiny of a Salford schoolteacher or employer. "I was off [work] for a fortnight."[16]

The Terence Rattigan tale would become an essential part of the Delaney myth, repeated *ad infinitum* in many a subsequent profile. Rattigan himself appeared to see the amusing side of it. He told a show business writer in 1959: "Mr Rattigan is being unusually cagey about the plot of his [new] play. When asked, he retorted wryly, 'It's all about sex in Salford. Miss Shelagh Delaney, the *dear* girl, has said she wrote *A Taste of Honey* after deciding that she must be able to write a better play than my last effort. Well, I think I can write a better play about sex in Salford than Miss Delaney, the *dear* girl … '"[17]

In fact, it was rather fashionable at the time to denigrate Rattigan. *Variation on a Theme*, covertly about a homosexual relationship, had toured the country in early 1958 before opening at the Globe Theatre in London on 8th May. It was a failure, the first flop in this gifted playwright's career.

For the aspiring 'progressive' writer, however, Rattigan represented all that was currently *passé* and outmoded about British theatre. Two years earlier, in 1956, John Osborne's play *Look Back in Anger* had rocked the theatrical establishment, and Rattigan's work looked tired and conventional as a consequence.

It's instructive to listen to the critic John Russell Taylor describing the mood of the late 1950s where budding writers were concerned, following the success of Osborne's play. "What is important about *Look Back in Anger* is the success it enjoyed and the consequences this had for a whole generation of writers; writers who fifty, fifteen, or even five years before would probably have adopted the novel as their chosen form but now, all of a sudden, were moved to try their hand at drama and, even more surprisingly, found companies to stage their works and audiences to appreciate them … where the ultimate success was not so long ago a best-selling novel, now it was a hit play."[18]

Or, to put it more simply, as Delaney did in 1959, "'I'm interested in writing plays at the moment because there's more of a kick in writing them than writing novels, isn't there? I once started to write a book,' she said, 'but that's where it ended up', pointing to the fireplace."[19]

It would have been impossible for a young person interested in contemporary theatre not to have been aware of *Look Back in Anger* and the 'Angry Young Men' movement then currently capturing the literary headlines. Though she would later claim to have hated *Look Back in Anger*, having seen it on television, John Osborne's sudden rise to fame can only have enthused her.

That Delaney enjoyed playing down her educational achievements, portraying herself as a rough, unlettered diamond, the product of a flawed educational system, was obvious. Though she boasted about not being 'an intellectual', all these traits are understandable in a young woman, keen to shape herself, to *create* herself, as it were. Thus, her insouciant comments concerning Osborne and Sagan can be seen as unreliable. She was sharper and shrewder than she let on.

Indeed, her decision to send her work to Joan Littlewood at Stratford East reveals a very canny young mind at work. The play's appearance on Joan Littlewood's doorstep certainly intrigued the veteran director even before she'd opened the package:

> The play was in a packet postmarked 'Salford', where I'd lived with Jimmie Miller [Ewan McColl] when I was nineteen, the same age as this girl. Everybody was poor there and everybody seemed to be Scottish, Welsh or Irish. Hadn't there been a Delaney family opposite the Richmonds in Hartington Street when Gerry lodged there?[20]

Indeed there had.

NOTES

1  Joan Littlewood, *Joan's Book: Joan Littlewood's Peculiar History as She Tells It*. new edn (Methuen, 2003) hereafter cited as *Joan's Book*.
2  *Daily Mail*, 9th February 1959, the Robert Muller interview: 'The Lucretia Borgia of Salford Lancs.'
3  *Saturday Review*, 6th July 1963.
4  *The Times*, 2nd February 1959.
5  *Daily Mail*, 9th February 1959.
6  *The Times*, 2nd February 1959.
7  Ibid.
8  Interview with the author, 2013.
9  Ibid.
10  Ibid.
11  http://www.suttonelms.org.uk/sdelaney.html Diversity Website.
12  Interview with the author, 2013.
13  *Daily Mail*, 26th May 1958.
14  *Daily Mail*, 9th February 1959, (Robert Muller interview).
15  *Manchester Guardian*, 4th August 1976.
16  *The Times*, 2nd February 1959.
17  *Daily Express*, 'Inside Show Business', 18th February, 1959.
18  J.R. Taylor, *The Angry Theatre* (Hill & Wang, 1962), p. 9.
19  *Daily Mail*, 9th February 1959.
20  *Joan's Book*.

*Top:* Street in Brindle Heath, Salford, where Shelagh lived in the 1950s, taken in 1963 by Harold Riley.
*Bottom:* Shelagh (far right) at friend and neighbour Shirley Evans' (far left) first wedding anniversary,
September 1958.

"**My dad used to tell us to be careful what we said when she was with us because he was sure she
was taking notes**" (Shirley Evans).

# 3

# Theatreland

Then down from Salford comes this splendid young
prophetess, who, with typical good sense, calls at the right
address among the conspirators in Stratford, E.5, who then
carry her voice into the heart of Theatreland.

**Colin MacInnes, *Encounter*, April 1959**

Shelagh Delaney's decision to send her play all the way to London rather
than try and have it produced nearer home might, at first glance, seem a
little odd. There was, after all, the perfectly respectable, well-thought-of
repertory company operating at the Manchester Library, somewhere she
was familiar with and where she was able to watch rehearsals whenever
she wished. However, the likelihood of something new and controversial
being staged there was remote. Interviewed in 1961, its director David
Scase responded to suggestions that the output of his company was
'conservative' by insisting that it was, "no use bringing new plays to the
theatre if you empty it in the process".[1] Finance and survival were key
considerations for theatres large and small in the United Kingdom during
these post-war years.

In 1960, according to the Arts Council, there were forty-four repertory
companies functioning in England not to mention innumerable little
theatres and other occasional amateur groups, but the majority were in
a shaky financial situation and found it difficult to balance the books.
Thus they would tend to put on popular, established plays, in part
because those who went to the theatre, even in industrial areas, were
middle-aged members of professional classes who wanted something
substantial for their money. Manchester's Library company was on a
sound financial footing and had earned a reputation for being one of the
most polished and efficient repertory companies in the land. Thus,
Shelagh must have calculated that her own piece of work would never see
the light of day in such a context so close to home.

In London her options were also equally few. In 1958, London's theatre world looked utterly different from what exists today. There was the West End theatreland, of course, where commercial success was everything and 'experimental' theatre utterly non-existent. Beyond Shaftesbury Avenue, however, the theatrical landscape of any kind was bleak.

State funding for the theatre through subsidies was then in its infancy. The Arts Council had been founded in 1946 and had a certain amount of money to spend, but it would not be until 1963 that the National Theatre was established at the Old Vic, while the Olivier Theatre on the South Bank would only be completed in 1976. The Royal Shakespeare Company had yet to become a permanent organisation: that would happen in 1961. Bernard Miles' permanent Mermaid Theatre at Puddle Dock was still in the process of being constructed while smaller independent theatres such as the pre-war Gate and Q Theatres had disappeared, the victims of financial blight.

There existed the tiny Arts Theatre, in Great Newport Street in London's West End, a membership-supported club that took risks by producing new, experimental, unlicensed plays that were thought to be commercially non-viable on the West End stage. In August 1955, for instance, 24-year-old Peter Hall directed the English-language premiere of Samuel Beckett's *Waiting for Godot* there. Such an 'intellectual' venue would have been anathema to Delaney.

That left two independent venues existing outside the West End: the Royal Court in Sloane Square hosting the English Stage Company (ESC) and the Theatre Royal in Stratford East, the home of the Theatre Workshop company. Both institutions would come to play a significant role in Delaney's creative life during the 1960s.

The ESC had been formed in 1954 uniting two disparate groups of people in a common cause. In 1953, the budding theatre directors George Devine and Tony Richardson were seeking a venue in London at which to present the whole range of contemporary drama with a small permanent company. They'd hoped to base it at the Royal Court Theatre, then newly acquired by a former music-hall performer, Alfred Esdaile, but the scheme foundered through lack of funds.

At about the same time the verse dramatist Ronald Duncan and his friends Lord Harewood and Edward Blacksell began corresponding with Esdaile's general manager, Oscar Lewenstein, about a London venue for experimental work and the establishment of a company to produce it. The English Stage Society was thus formed in 1954 (and became the English Stage Company soon afterwards) with a governing council of what were termed "stable, respected men in whom the Arts Council tends to place confidence". These included, among others, Esdaile himself and the textile industrialist Neville Blond, a powerful and influential businessman whose father-in-law had founded Marks & Spencer. In February 1956, the ESC bought the lease of the Royal Court Theatre in Sloane Square from Esdaile. Lewenstein, also on the ESC Council, suggested Devine should be approached to be the Artistic Director and thus began one of the most unlikely combinations in theatre history.

In the first draft of his unfinished autobiography, Devine wrote of his mission: "I was not strictly after a popular theatre ... but a theatre that would be part of the intellectual life of the country ... I was convinced the way to achieve my objective was to get writers, writers of serious pretensions, back into the theatre. This I set out to do. I wanted to change the attitude of the public towards the theatre ... "[2] They placed an advertisement in the *Stage* magazine asking for new plays. Their fourth production, in mid-1956, would be John Osborne's *Look Back in Anger*, the 'big bang' of post-war theatrical history. Under Devine's direction the English Stage Company would remain primarily a 'writer's theatre', placing the writer at the centre of events ostensibly to distinguish it from the West End, where plays were often nothing more than flimsy vehicles for 'celebrity' performers to entice undiscriminating middle-class audiences.

The formation and ethos of the Theatre Workshop could not have been more different. Its principal lights, Joan Littlewood and Ewan MacColl, had been resident in Manchester before the war, Littlewood as stage manager of the Rusholme Repertory company, MacColl working with the Clarion Players in his home city of Salford where he later formed his own agitprop group, the Red Megaphones. Both Littlewood and MacColl had been members of the Communist Party and, when founding their Theatre Union of Action in 1935, had written a manifesto that stated: "Politics, in its fullest sense, means the affairs of the people. In this sense, the plays done will be political."[3]

For MacColl, in particular, theatre became his method of interacting with the political struggle: "I really did want to tear down the world in which I found myself, and build a new world."[4]

After the war, the pair formed the Theatre Workshop and, short of money and unable to secure a suitable building of their own, they and their company toured the English provinces putting on productions of Molière and Chekhov mixed in with original material by MacColl. The latter pieces were used as focal points for ensemble improvisations during performances. Littlewood herself made several adaptations from Charles Dickens, Lewis Carroll, Robert Louis Stevenson and Honoré de Balzac. Though critically praised for their work, they found the endless touring exhausting and the monetary returns scarce.

In 1953 the company arrived in Stratford, East London, and leased the Theatre Royal, an old run-down music hall, for six months. Before their arrival, the show running at the Royal had been a striptease revue, *Jane of the Daily Mirror*.

Neither Littlewood nor MacColl actually wanted to be in London. In his 1990 autobiography MacColl stated: "It was plain that we had reached the point where we would either have to disband or find another way of working … Our aims could not be achieved by touring, at least not unless we were subsidized. We had made countless appeals to a deaf Arts Council; we had approached trade unions and government agencies … And we had gone on working, postponing the inevitable decision. Now it could no longer be postponed. We had to put down roots."[5]

Littlewood, in spite of her London background (she was born in Stockwell, south London), had no sense of returning to her roots. "I hate London; it's the Calcutta of the north," she said in 1994. "I love Manchester and tried like hell to settle in Glasgow; but it was the only theatre we could get for £20 a week. I detested the dump; it stank."[6]

Both in their origins and in outlook, Theatre Workshop in the East and the Royal Court in the West were thus divided by more than just the City of London. Indeed, there existed from the beginning a fierce rivalry, especially keen from Littlewood's point of view. For Littlewood theatre was important to communal well-being, particularly of the working class, "in a market economy dominated by a commercial theatre in which they were not encouraged to take part and which reflected middle and upper class tastes".

Philosophically and politically, she wanted to be independent of the 'establishment' in order to create a truly alternative theatre based on the fact that, as she admitted late in her life, "I've always been a communist. I know things go wrong, of course they do. But we didn't go wrong. We didn't sell out."[7]

George Devine at the Royal Court, on the other hand, wrote: "I was not strictly after a popular theatre à la Joan Littlewood–Roger Planchon, but a theatre that would be part of the intellectual life of the country."[8]

Critic and cultural historian John Russell Taylor agreed: "It seems to me obvious that, whatever his private political views might be, George Devine never wanted to found a politically-oriented theatre, and never had any clearly defined idea of what function his company ought to exercise in society beyond providing all playgoers with the best drama it could lay its hands on in whatever shape or form interesting writers liked to write it."[9]

Since *Look Back in Anger*, the Royal Court had succeeded in launching new and radically minded writers. There had been John Osborne's two follow-up plays, *The Entertainer* and *Epitaph for George Dillon*; John Arden's *The Waters of Babylon*; Ann Jellicoe's *The Sport of My Mad Mother*; novelist Doris Lessing's *Each His Own Wilderness*; plus Arnold Wesker's *Chicken Soup with Barley*.

However, after the first couple of years it was noted that the ESC had not, as it had originally claimed it would, created a permanent repertory with a regular core of actors. It was, to some observers, starting to behave like any other West End theatre, relying on big names such as Laurence Olivier and Joan Plowright to lure in the crowds. Its ethos, though striving hard to be 'left-wing' was still very much middle-class with its directors and writers drawn largely from a top university- and public school-educated elite.

By 1961, George Devine was having to answer charges about the Royal Court's safe and uncontroversial programming. He gave the game away when admitting: "We knew that to be accepted by the middle, to be smiled upon by the top, is the first sweet kiss of death. So we carry on flirting with death in order to live."[10]

In other words, commercial sponsors and grants from the Arts Council played a crucial part in determining how the theatre operated.

By stark contrast, throughout its tenure in Stratford the Theatre Workshop would live from hand to mouth. Its initial financial support came from a supporters' club which raised a certain amount of money by promoting Ewan MacColl's 'Ballad and Blues' evenings and club performances of plays. Otherwise the company members sometimes found themselves in the embarrassing position of having to make appeals from the stage after each show and even installing a collection box in the foyer.

Whereas the Arts Council tended to look with some favour on the ESC, it merely frowned on the Theatre Workshop. Theatre Workshop's first Arts Council subsidy of £150 would be received in 1952. This would be raised to £500 for the following two years and £1,000 in each of three subsequent years. It's been calculated that between 1958 and 1963, the ESC would receive some £46,500. By contrast, the Theatre Workshop would be handed little more than £9,000. Those 'stable, respected men' on the Royal Court's governing council were clearly very effective.

Joan Littlewood attributed the disparity in treatment to the fact that "the Arts Council … have never believed that a theatre could be a success anywhere but in a respectable middle-class district, and our survival for ten years without their help and for the last three years with their tiny grant has been a source of amazement, if not irritation, to them. We couldn't even get £50 out of the Arts Council when the gas was being cut off. We applied for grants and they called us East End savages and reds and asked us if we knew anything about the Laurence Olivier seasons at the Old Vic."[11]

Theatre Workshop designer John Bury agreed: "In the early days, we were regarded as a bunch of Reds. Moscow Gold and all that stuff. At Stratford East, I think it was the lack of accountability that worried them. There was a lot of fuss about the [account] books and keeping it together, programming and playing. Joan would always be rude to them. We didn't play their game and they weren't going to play ours. They felt if we wanted to behave like that we could run our own theatre. Then they gave us a bit, but we were always well below the Royal Court. Joan expected money from the Arts Council on trust, but she didn't get it."[12]

The references to Moscow and 'Reds' had substance. According to Ben Harker, "The Arts Council's refusal properly to subsidize the company has been long been linked to Theatre Workshop's radical, anti-establishment and counter-hegemonic tendencies."[13] During the war, Joan Littlewood had been banned from broadcasting because of her communist proclivities and advocacy of left-wing ideas. The BBC lifted the ban two years later when MI5 said she had broken off her association with the Communist Party. However, MI5 continued to keep her under surveillance even after Theatre Workshop moved to Stratford. Thus, "The lines of communication were forever open between MI5, the BBC and other institutions of cultural authority."[14]

Indeed, in 1954, during surveillance of MacColl and Theatre Workshop, MI5 apparently heard that that the author of their current play had recently received a large royalty cheque from the Soviet Union and that members of the Theatre Workshop were drunk for an entire evening celebrating on the proceeds![15]

It must also be said, however, that Joan Littlewood herself did nothing to ease the situation. "She lived by the maxim that it is the duty of artists to bite the hand that feeds them."[16]

As we will see, Delaney was, even as a young girl, distinctly leftward-leaning. Kitchin of *The Times* wrote: "The relationship with her father, who died last July, leads back to a Socialist grandfather of the Keir Hardie tradition and forward to the welfare state, which provided her education, in a uniquely British social pattern."[17] In time, she would come to have an MI5 file all to herself. For now, the anti-intellectual ethos of the Theatre Workshop would have been a welcoming feature. But there were other reasons for Shelagh gravitating east London-wards.

In May 1956, a few weeks after *Look Back in Anger* began to create a storm, Theatre Workshop also had had a big hit of its own with a play by a new, unheralded Irish playwright, Brendan Behan.

His play, *The Quare Fellow*, was about a man waiting to be executed and it would go on to achieve a profitable West End run at the Comedy Theatre but not until Behan himself gained instant notoriety on prime-time BBC television. During a promotional event for the West End opening of the play, Behan appeared drunk in an interview with Malcolm Muggeridge, a prominent journalist, author and media personality. Behan had insisted on going on, despite attempts to prevent him, because he wished to insult the English public by shouting obscenities at the cameras. At Television Centre, Muggeridge and various BBC officials attempted and failed to sober him up: without the stimulus of further drinks, he sank into a glazed semi-coma, and said nothing.[18] Such things simply never happened in those early days of live television and Behan became an instant celebrity. A radio play by him called *The Big House* was another success in 1957, and 1958 saw his novel *Borstal Boy* published to great acclaim.

As we've seen, Shelagh was immensely proud of her Irish roots. She was also a great fan of Behan's work and would gravitate towards him both professionally and emotionally immediately she reached London.

Finally, there was the Theatre Workshop's overtly campaigning nature, particularly in the field of censorship, which was then a crucial issue in any writer's life.

In the year Delaney was writing her first play, Theatre Workshop was fighting a battle with the censors housed at the Lord Chamberlain's office. Until the Theatres Act of 1968, which saw the end of stage censorship, all plays had to be officially licensed from the offices, and the 'banned' list included nudity, swearwords, risqué stage business, representations of God, the Royal Family, anyone living, or homosexuality – and no actor and actress could appear together in bed under the same sheet.

In October 1957, the actor Richard Harris was appearing in a Theatre Workshop play called *You Won't Always Be on Top*, set on a building-site. Harris apparently put a watering can between his legs, raised his fingers in the V-sign and, in Churchillian tones, said: 'I declare this site open.'

His performance was deemed to have, 'defamed a living legend', and was thus contrary to section 15 of the Theatres Act 1843. Not only Harris but the Theatre Workshop manager, Gerry Raffles, director Joan Littlewood and the playwright Henry Chapman all appeared in court. A fighting fund was set up; the Manchester-born MP, Harold Lever, who had been business manager of Manchester's Theatre Union, Littlewood's original theatre group, in 1938, defended them and in January 1958 they won a moral victory. Their fine was minimal, and the *cause célèbre* was reported in every national newspaper along with pictures of the cast celebrating in a local public house. It can be no coincidence that Delaney sent her play to the Theatre Workshop a few weeks later.

On 9th May 1958, the *Salford City Reporter* ran an article beneath the headline, 'Girl's First Play To Be Produced'.

> Miss Shelagh Delaney aged 19 of Duchy Road, a photographer's assistant, has had her first play accepted by the London experimental group Theatre Workshop which hopes to produce it later this month. The group has also taken a two years option on her further work. The play is called *A Touch of Honey* [*sic*] and is described as a modern romance based on the relationship between a mother and a daughter.
>
> Mr G. Raffles, manager of the group, said, "We have had 2,500 plays sent to us in the last five years and this is only the fourth we have accepted. The love scenes are amazingly frank and a scene between the girl and a Negro boy is brilliantly written." Brunette-haired Shelagh told the *City Reporter:* "I'm delighted to get my first play accepted – it's proved what I thought. But I'm not building my hopes too much in case it's a flop."[19]

It was the first time the paper had mentioned her and it would certainly not be the last.

NOTES

1 David Scase, *Manchester Guardian*, 16th October 1961.
2 *IMDb*, Mini Biography by Jon C. Hopwood.
3 Howard Goorney, *The Theatre Workshop Story* (Methuen Publishing Ltd, 2008).
4 Raphael Samuel, Ewan MacColl and Stuart Cosgrove, *Theatres of the Left, 1880–1935: Workers' Theatre Movements in Britain and America* (Routledge & Kegan Paul, 1985), p. 213.
5 Ewan MacColl, *Journeyman: An Autobiography* introduction by Peggy Seeger (Sidgwick & Jackson, 1990).
6 Joan Littlewood, 'Making a Scene', *Independent Magazine,* 26th March 1994.

7   D. Keith Peacock, *Changing Performance: Culture and Performance in the British Theatre since 1945* (Peter Lang, 2007), p. 82.

8   Irving Wardle, *The Theatres of George Devine* (Jonathan Cape, 1978).

9   John Russell Taylor, '*Ten Years of the English Stage Company*', *Drama Review*, 11, 2 (Winter, 1969).

10  Gregory Motton, *Helping Themselves: The Leftwing Middle Classes in the Theatre and the Arts* (Levellers Press, 2009).

11  Littlewood, 'Making a Scene'.

12  Goorney, *The Theatre Workshop Story*.

13  Ben Harker, 'Missing Dates: Theatre Workshop', *History Workshop*,  66, 1 (2008), pp. 272–9.

14  Ibid.

15  Ibid.

16  Peacock, *Changing Performance*.

17  *The Times*, 2nd February 1959.

18  http://www.nybooks.com/articles/archives/1966/feb/03/dylan-thomas/?pagination=false

19  *SCR*, 9th May 1958.

# 4

## *A Taste of Honey*

*A Taste of Honey* is a two-act play divided into four scenes set in Salford, Lancashire in the 1950s. The title Shelagh explained, " ... which everybody at one time in their lives experiences – comes from the Bible where Jonathan says to Saul, 'And Jonathan told him, and said, *I did but taste a little honey with the end of the rod that* was *in my hand, and, lo, I must die?*'"[1]

It concerns Jo, a seventeen-year-old working-class girl and her mother Helen. Helen is described as a 'semi-whore' in one published version of the script, but Delaney has said elsewhere, "The mother is not a prostitute, I have nowhere said that she is – would she have kept her daughter with her if she had been? She is just a woman who enjoys life and goes about it in her own way. The bad effect she has on Jo – and on Geof – is not due to malice or cruelty, but to sheer lack of thought about other people. A scatter-brained woman who can never find her hat or shoes."[1]

Helen and Jo have a confrontational and ambiguously interdependent relationship. Between the two of them there exists a very real bond although it often expresses itself in mutual recrimination.

In the first scene of Act I, they enter a shabby bed-sitting room for the first time, bickering and point-scoring off one another. They have not unpacked, and Helen has a bad cold. She complains about this throughout the scene, all the while sniping at Jo's inefficiency and incompetence. At odd moments, Helen addresses the audience, turning away from the action to make remarks such as "She can't do a thing for herself, that girl," and, "You bring them up and they turn round and talk to you like that."

Jo looks about the room, criticising it and making small, futile attempts to brighten it up. She tries to cover the bare light-bulb with a handkerchief and burns her hand; she brings out some flower bulbs she has stolen from a local park and looks for somewhere to place them; she seeks out the bathroom and the kitchen, where she turns on the gas causing a small explosion.

There are references to Helen's sexual appetite, to her love of singing in public houses and the fact that she appears to be running away from something. Helen notices some drawings of Jo's and tries to hang them up ("I didn't realise I had such a talented daughter"). She offers to pay for Jo to go to art school, but Jo says it's too late: she wants to get a job and a place of her own. Their mutual sniping carries with it a comical undertone, Jo expressing scorn at her mother's attempts to present herself as an attractive woman. She is also resentful of the way their itinerant lifestyle has placed her at a disadvantage in life. Helen is dismissive of Jo's concerns ("I know, I'm a cruel, wicked woman"). Jo says, "I've had enough of school. Too many different schools and too many different places."

Their squabbling is interrupted by the arrival of Peter, described in the play text as "a brash car salesman, cigar in mouth". Peter is an ex-lover of Helen's, a much younger man and very keen on sex. His discovery that Helen has a daughter surprises him momentarily, but Jo is sent to the kitchen to make some coffee. Helen and Peter then start a conversation in which it is revealed that Helen has run away from him, ostensibly because she is tired of their life together. Out of the blue, Peter offers to marry her, a casual, throwaway gesture ("You won't find anything better"), though perhaps the result Helen has been aiming at. Jo re-enters with the coffee and Peter continues to press his offer on Helen. When made aware of it, Jo is scornful. Peter then leaves to allow Helen to deal with her cold, and mother and daughter prepare to go to bed. Jo then confesses to being afraid of the dark and reveals deeper problems: "I'm not frightened of the darkness outside. It's the darkness inside houses I don't like."

In the second scene of Act I, we find Jo outdoors in the street with a black sailor, apparently her boyfriend but identified in the script simply as 'Boy'. They kiss and he asks her to marry him in similar fashion to Peter's proposal to Helen. She accepts, also light-heartedly, and they suggest the marriage will occur on his next shore leave in six months' time. She ties the ring he gives her to a ribbon she has worn in her hair and hangs it round her neck. Their interchanges have a current 'pop-song' ring to them ("I don't know why I love you but I do") with joking references to cannibals and the jungle ("Mau Mau – matrimony"). The

Boy also refers to her as 'Honey' and there are several amusing, resonant lines (*Jo*: I love you. *Boy*: Why? *Jo*: Because you're daft). He waves goodbye, turns and sings to the audience, and goes.

We are back in the bedsit. Helen dances to music, lies down and reads an evening paper. Jo dances on dreamily. Helen quickly senses that Jo has been seeing a boy. The two then consider going to the cinema and, scanning the newspaper, they look at a picture of a bosomy actress. Jo says, "I'd sooner be put on't streets. It's more honest." Helen tells Jo that she was divorced by her first husband because she had Jo with another man. She then reveals she is getting married again. After mother and daughter exchange insults, Peter arrives with flowers. He and Helen are going out to dinner. As Helen changes her clothes, Peter and Jo lock horns and Jo makes a few brief, semi-serious attempts to flirt with Peter ("Do you fancy me?"), and she questions him about his reactions to Helen: ("Do you fancy her?" and "Do you think Helen's beautiful?" and "Am I like her?"). She is apparently relieved that there seems to be no resemblance between herself and her mother, but she concludes with a petulant "Leave me alone and leave my mother alone, too."

Helen re-enters and shows Jo a picture of Peter's new house. When she leaves the room, Jo spots pictures of various other women Peter keeps in his wallet; she then asks to see the hole where his missing eye was. There exists a sort of playfulness between them, with Jo demonstrating a rivalry with Helen. Peter gives her a cigarette.

It seems Helen and Peter may be going away for a weekend, that they may well marry and go off on a honeymoon. Jo is, despite her earlier defiant aggression, clearly upset. Helen and Peter depart. The Boy then appears. Jo is now suffering from a cold and he starts to fix her a cold cure. During the ensuing conversation Shakespeare's *Othello* is invoked. Jo asks the Boy to stay, knowing that it will lead to nothing positive for herself. They embrace.

The scene fades, and Helen reappears, dressing to get married. She spots the ring hanging round Jo's neck and Jo admits the 'Boy' has asked her to marry him. Helen scolds her and appears for the first time to be showing some maternal sympathy ("Why don't you learn from my mistakes?"). As Helen is preparing to go, Jo asks about her father and Helen reveals that he was "Not very bright" and that he is dead. Helen leaves and Jo calls out, "Good Luck, Helen."

Act II opens some months later in summer and inside the same room as before. Jo enters with a different young man, Geof and she is clearly pregnant. She asks him why he has been thrown out of his own room, the

Start of Act II

implication being that he is homosexual. She demands to know about "people like you". She wants to know what they 'do'. He refuses to say and makes to leave but she asks him to stay, apologising. He then criticises her drawings (he is an art student) and she discusses her plight and her pregnancy. Geof asks her about her mother but Jo reveals her deeper fears declaring, "The baby'll be born dead or daft!" Geof reassures her, they chatter, establish a friendship, then retire for the night in separate beds. She sings the song 'Black Boy' and tells Geof that the father of her baby was black, "From darkest Africa! A Prince."

The scene moves on a month or two later, and Jo is watching poorly dressed and dirty children playing outside. Geof is making a dress for the impending child. Jo alternates between happiness and anguish, and taunts Geof for his lack of confidence. She reiterates her hatred of motherhood and when Geof suggests they form a relationship, Jo says, "You're nothing to me. I'm everything to myself." Though she suggests he leaves, he declares he is going to stay. At this point, Helen appears. She confronts Jo about her pregnancy and appears unsympathetic. There follows a long argument, with Helen insisting that Jo get some exercise and pull herself together. At its height, Geof tells them both to shut up and they turn on him, so he goes off to make tea.

Helen insists on paying for Jo's upkeep, but Jo is scornful. Peter then appears. He is very drunk and makes sarcastic remarks and sings bawdy songs. There is something unpleasant about his mirth that hints at a possible break-up between himself and Helen. When he leaves the room, Jo and Helen talk, but as Helen offers Jo a place in her home Peter reappears and rejects the idea, even threatening to throw Helen out. Throughout this sequence there are many rude references directed towards Geof regarding his apparent homosexuality. Helen momentarily decides to stay with Jo, but when Jo rejects her she leaves. No money has been left.

Scene 2 opens some months later with Jo and Geof still in the flat and the baby imminent. Geof is cleaning. The flower bulbs Jo originally brought to the room are dead. The two young people console one another and Jo talks of how her mother rejected her. Geof says Jo is like Helen and she tells him of her father. Geof reassures her, suggesting that Helen was lying about the "feeble-mindedness" of the man. They talk about the coming birth and Geof brings out a toy doll for her to practise changing nappies on, but Jo petulantly throws it away declaring she doesn't want the child, nor does she want a man. They calm down, make tea, and seem happy together.

Helen then enters with her baggage. She fusses over Jo, asking her if she's packed ready for the hospital. It appears that she has been thrown out by Peter but she insists that she came back in time to help with the baby. She bullies and insults Geof into leaving the room. Jo goes to lie down and Helen then confronts Geof. She drives him away and he leaves, insisting that Helen should not frighten Jo. When Jo awakes, she imagines that Geof is still in the flat. Jo then tells Helen the child will be black and Helen, shocked, leaves to get a drink. The play ends with Jo singing one of the nursery rhymes that Geof sang to her earlier in the play.

As we shall see, the text and structure of Delaney's original play script were altered considerably by Joan Littlewood and her Theatre Workshop company. However, she had sent her play to Stratford in the knowledge that it dealt with controversial themes. As John Bay commented drily, "Teenage sex, a black baby on the way and a queer boyfriend. She's not so dumb."[2]

She would have been well aware that, before it could be performed, it would be necessary for it to be submitted to the Lord Chamberlain's office. However, she would have expected Theatre Workshop to fight her corner.

In many ways, she was lucky. By the time the play was submitted on 2nd May 1958, the censors were having to take cognisance of a significant development in the nation's approach to sex and morality. Sir John Wolfenden's Report of the Committee on Homosexuality and Prostitution, published in September 1957, had, amongst other recommendations, suggested that homosexual behaviour between consenting adults in private should no longer be a criminal offence. The report itself would not be acted upon officially for another ten years but the then Lord Chamberlain, Lord Scarbrough, noted, "it was bound to appear absurd to quite sensible people to disallow any attempt to deal seriously with a subject which had now become, unfortunately, one of the problems of life."[3] Whether by accident or design, *A Taste of Honey* would be the first important test of how far the theatre censors had actually changed their outlook regarding the depiction of homosexuality.

The Lord Chamberlain's assistant, a Brigadier Norman Gwatkin, having read the play, was adamant: "I think it's revolting, quite apart from the homosexual bits To me it has no saving grace whatsoever. If we pass muck like this, it does give our critics something to go on."[4]

However, the Lord Chamberlain's chief play-reader, Charles Heriot, thought it, "a surprisingly good play … though, God knows, it is not to my personal taste." Where the vexed matter of homosexuality was concerned, he thought, "Geof, is delicately conveyed", although he felt the scenes where Geof, "explains his position in society to Jo, and Helen calls him a pervert and a castrated little clown" can "easily come out".

He concluded: "The point I wish to make is that this play is balanced on a knife edge. It is the perfect borderline case, since it is concerned with the forbidden subject in a way that no one, I believe, could take exception to. In my opinion, therefore, it is recommended for licence but I think that the Comptroller and the Lord Chamberlain should both read the play carefully themselves."[5]

The Lord Chamberlain agreed. The word 'castrated' was removed and Geof's self-revelatory speech to Jo was toned down to lessen "the suggestion of homosexuality". On 15th May, a licence was issued "on the understanding the omissions are made".[6]

After the play's opening on 27th May, Theatre Workshop felt obliged to return the play for further consideration as changes had occurred to the original during rehearsals, but as nothing had been added regarding Geof's homosexuality, the play was passed once again.

Later in the same year the ban on homosexual subjects on stage was lifted but, as Anthony Aldgate has noted, "It was tardily achieved, not easily forthcoming, nor readily welcomed in all quarters."[7] Clearly a complete ban could no longer be sustained, but it was also felt that the Lord Chamberlain could still not allow complete liberty on the subject. Thus, it was laid down that no physical contact between homosexuals would be allowed, the subject had be treated 'seriously' and homosexual characters would only be allowed to appear if they were 'necessary to the action and theme' of the play. In other words, they had to earn their right to exist, fictionally speaking!

It has subsequently been claimed that Delaney's portrayal of Geof was ground-breaking in that, until *A Taste of Honey*, playwrights had tried to evade the censor's veto by resorting to subterfuge and innuendo. Nicholas de Jongh wrote: "It is highly probable that Delaney's treatment of the subject and the favourable critical and public response to *A Taste of Honey* played a significant role in persuading the Lord Chamberlain partially to relax his ban on homosexuality and gays a few months later. Shelagh Delaney ought to rank as a gay heroine."[8]

Murray Melvin, who played Geof on stage in the original production, certainly thought so: "I played a gay person not as a figure of fun – which was the norm for gay characters in 1957, but as a character with dignity."[9]

It has even been claimed that Delaney wrote her play, not as a protest at the vapidity of Rattigan's middle-class commercial vehicle *Variation on a Theme*, but as a direct riposte to his treatment of homosexuality in the play. That may be overstating the case, however.

That Geof made efforts to establish a heterosexual relationship with Jo probably redeemed him, somewhat, in the censors' eyes. They could see that Geof's sexual orientation threatened no one. In fact, he hardly possessed a sexual identity at all, being more a eunuch than a homosexual, hence the scorn with which he was treated by both Helen and Peter, and even Jo herself.

Dan Rebellato thought Geof, "a very strange homosexual. For much of the play he seems more interested in trying to start a relationship with Jo. He is certainly cut off from the queer community, and thus has little to counter his descriptions as a 'pansified little freak', a 'bloody little pansy', an old woman, 'that queer' etc. The only New Wave queers allowed on stage were like Geoffrey Ingham, shorn of their subversive performativity – *their queerness*."[10]

 Joss Bennathan has noted: "Indeed it is significant that, although Jo questions Geof about what he does with other men, no reference is made to his lovers and he is kept away from any sexual activity during the action of the play."[11]

Given the straitjacket into which the censors had strapped homosexual characters following their partial lifting of the ban, however, it would have been impossible to have taken Geof's sexual life – such as it was – any further than Delaney managed. There is also the fact, as de Jongh noted, 'gay communities' were thin on the ground in 1958. Geof's confusion about his sexuality mirrors that of many gay young men (and women) adrift and alone in those pre-liberated days.

Homosexuality aside, the censors were relatively kind to the text, concerned only occasionally by certain 'colourful' phrases and insisting, for instance, that a line referring to Helen ("Worn out but still a good few pumps left in her") be dropped.

Some time later, before the play was transferred to the West End, a member of the public wrote to the Lord Chamberlain complaining about the "appalling use of blasphemy in the dialogue". Gwatkin replied that it was difficult "with a play of this type", to delete all passages that might offend. He wrote, somewhat forlornly: "The Lord Chamberlain feels that whilst there are passages which will be objectionable, as they have proved to you, they are in character in this sordid and melancholy play. To live, the theatre must be a mirror to contemporary life in its good and bad aspects, and the Lord Chamberlain is of the opinion that because it depicts such a sad collection of undesirables it will not do the public any harm."[12]

When the play burst onto the Theatre Workshop's Stratford stage, however, "sordid and melancholy" would not be the words the majority of those in attendance would use to describe it.

NOTES

1 Methuen Student edition of *A Taste of Honey* (1982).

2 *Joan's Book.*

3 The following quotations are taken from Anthony Aldgate, *Censorship and the Permissive Society: British Cinema and Theatre 1955–1965* (Clarendon Press, 1995), pp. v–viii and ch. 6, 'A Woman's Lot', which examines the compromises reached in *A Taste of Honey.*

4 Ibid.

5 Ibid.

6 Ibid.

7 Ibid.

8 *Guardian*, 25th November 2011: 'Taste of Honey Led to End of Gay Ban'.

9 Interview with Murray Melvin at the Royal Exchange Theatre, November 2004. http://www.royalexchange.co.uk.

10 Dan Rebellato, 'Something Unspoken', in *1956 and All That: The Making of Modern British Drama* (Routledge, 1999).

11 Joss Bennathan, 'Delaney, Shelagh', in K.A. Berney and N.G. Templeton (eds.), *Contemporary British Dramatists* (St James Press, 1994), pp. 185–7.

12 Aldgate, *Censorship and the Permissive Society.*

# 5

# Littlewood's Workshop

We are both creatures of Joan's imagination, said Brendan
Behan to Shelagh Delaney. "Perhaps they were", agreed
Littlewood.

The *Guardian*, September 2002

There can't have been many successful playwrights in theatrical history
(Shakespeare perhaps aside!) who have found their work clinically
dissected in order to discover exactly how much of it was theirs and how
much someone else's. Theatre Workshop director Joan Littlewood was
always forthright about her own contribution to the shaping and
presentation of the play. In her autobiography and in various subsequent
interviews in newspapers she insisted that the original manuscript was
ill-shaped and largely incoherent as a piece of work. She recognised there
were lots of good lines and some "funny, quirky expressions", as she later
described them, plus a couple of believable characters but that the plot
was non-existent. She summed it up thus: "Helen, a woman of forty, goes
off with her rather unbelievable boyfriend, leaving her daughter, Jo, to
spend Christmas alone. Jo goes to bed with a young Nigerian sailor who
soon disappears. Some months later, Geof, an effeminate art student,
moves in, sleeps on the couch and takes care of the girl, who is now
pregnant. That was about all there was to it."[1]

Nevertheless, she felt it was worth salvaging. She would treat the
material as the "basis for a sort of commedia dell'arte improvisation"
and "with some brilliant people, we made it into a play". She felt she had
the actors to do it and she thus set about persuading them. Avis Bunnage
was one of them. Ardwick-born Bunnage was a Theatre Workshop
veteran, having given up previous jobs as a secretary and nursery teacher
in 1947 to join Chorlton Repertory Theatre in Manchester. She'd made
her first London appearance with the Theatre Workshop Company in
1952 and acted in many of its subsequent productions such as *An Enemy*

Joan Littlewood's view of Shelagh's script

*of the People, The Good Soldier Schweik, Mother Courage, The Italian Straw Hat, Captain Brassbound's Conversion* and *The Playboy of the Western World*. She and Littlewood were regularly at odds, however, and when approached to play the part of Helen in *A Taste of Honey*, Bunnage at first refused. She claimed many years later that she hadn't liked the play at all, that it 'wasn't playable' and that Shelagh Delaney, whom she'd never met, needed a 'swift kick up the arse'.[2]

This version of events has taken root in popular theatrical mythology, confirmed by occasional remarks made down the years by many of those in and around the Theatre Workshop at the time: that Littlewood had a "major hand in writing the play", that "she [JL] totally reshaped [what] was an early draft made by Shelagh", that it was "all a lot of notes which had to be turned into a play". The idea was even picked up on by one of Delaney's firmest critics at the time, the editor of the *Salford City Reporter*, who wrote in 1958, "What Shelagh did, of course, was to write a sort of rough sketch which was 'meaty' enough for the versatile players of an experimental group to get hold of and believe me some of the technical stunts they had to pull off to do it were hair-raising."[3]

There were dissenting voices, however. Frances Cuka, who would play Jo in the original stage version told Alec Patton when he asked her about Theatre Workshop's alterations to Delaney's script, "The best bits were hers."[4] While agreeing that there was a considerable amount of rewriting and a lot of improvisation using the original dialogue, not to mention some cutting of scenes, she felt that the play was essentially the one that Delaney had presented, the one that she had written on her battered old typewriter in Duchy Road.

The controversy led the well-known critic John Russell Taylor, whose seminal account of the period, *Anger and After*, was produced in 1966, to take an objective look at the original typescript and compare it with the performed version. He judged them "not so radically different" as most published comment would lead one to believe. He agreed that the character of Peter had been altered to increase his seediness: "Peter originally is a complete seventeen-year-old's dream figure of cosmopolitan sophistication, speaking throughout in a style of intricately throwaway cynicism. In the second act, however (in which, incidentally, his marriage to Helen seems to be working out quite satisfactorily), he reveals a child-loving heart of gold beneath the cynical exterior when, in an extraordinary scene just before he and Helen visit Jo, he suggests that they should take on the baby, and Jo, too, if she will come!"[5] Geof, meanwhile, had made more overt references to his homosexuality in the

*Top:* Joan Littlewood outside her Theatre Workshop in 1964.
*Bottom left:* Frances Cuka and Jimmie Moore, 1958.
*Bottom right:* Murray Melvin, Frances Cuka, John Bay and Avis Bunnage, 1958.

**"Some schoolgirl bollocks about a mother and her daughter's black bastard?"**
The original production of *A Taste of Honey* that shocked the theatre world of 1958.

original typescript. The ending had also been altered. The original had Helen sending Jo off to hospital to have the baby, planning to take her home afterwards and thus leaving Geof forlorn. "But", Taylor concluded, "most of the most celebrated lines are already there ... and the character of Jo, the play's raison d'être, is already completely created and unmistakably the same."[5]

Littlewood has clearly underplayed the value of the original script. As we will see, she would reject Shelagh's second play out of hand because she felt it lacked shape and purpose – and this was following the tremendous success of *A Taste of Honey*. It's certain that a seasoned professional such as Littlewood would never have taken such a risk on an unknown author, someone who had "written whatever had come into her head 'higgledy, piggledy'".[6] She was enthused enough with the play to drop the Workshop's next planned production, Bernard Kops' *The Hamlet of Stepney Green*, because she could see that *Honey* was something utterly new and fresh. Littlewood was, in fact, planning to close the theatre down, the financial situation having reached crisis point, and she sensed, quite correctly, that *A Taste of Honey* would be the perfect swansong.

Littlewood's memoirs have come in for a great deal of criticism for their point-scoring and for the way in which she downplayed certain individuals and their contributions to what was a glorious period in theatre history. But there is perhaps a simple reason why her recollections might appear so destructive to Delaney's initial achievement.

Theatre Workshop was, according to Stephen Lacey[7] "*different* from every other company operating in London in the mid-fifties, not simply because of the plays it produced, but also because of the *processes it employed to produce them*. The company was, in almost every area of its activities, an alternative to the then dominant forms of commercial theatre; instead of a clear division of labour between theatrical functions, the company valued critical discussion of texts and collaborative working methods."[8]

Littlewood also made it perfectly clear in 1965 what her priorities were and how she went about implementing them:

> I do not believe in the supremacy of the director, designer, actor or even the writer. It is through collaboration that this knockabout art of theatre survives and kicks ... No one mind or imagination can foresee what a play will become until all the physical and intellectual stimuli which are crystallized in the poetry of the author, have been understood by the company, and then tried out in terms of mime, discussion and the precise, music of grammar; words and movement allied and integrated.[9]

By choosing Delaney's play script, just as she had chosen another unknown writer's play – *The Quare Fellow* by Brendan Behan – to develop, she was making a definite statement about what theatre should be and how it should develop. The Irishman Behan and the Lancastrian Delaney represented voices emanating from the periphery of British society in terms of age, gender and class as well as region. Littlewood's production techniques as they had been evolving down the years set out to blur the boundaries of theatrical taste and form in a deliberate strategy of opposition to commercially orientated West End theatre as well as the middle-class 'writer's theatre' of the Royal Court.

As an avowed communist, albeit with a small 'c', Littlewood eschewed lauding the individual genius above the rest of theatrical humanity. In her new, populist theatre community, where everyone from the stage carpenters to the lighting men, from the cleaners to the prompts could participate in the development of an idea, it was necessary for the various egos of all concerned to be sacrificed to the common cause – particularly the writers. If they were comfortable with submitting their work to Littlewood's processes then there was a great deal to be gained, even though it meant relinquishing control and finding one's work being 're-worked' by actors in rehearsal, sometimes beyond recognition.

Brendan Behan, famously, was parked in the pub opposite the theatre during rehearsals of *The Quare Fellow* and only consulted when replacement lines were called for. Other playwrights objected. Frank Norman and Wolf Mankowitz, whose plays followed Delaney's on the Theatre Workshop production line, were more critical of her approach and resisted.

For Shelagh, it was a process she was ultimately happy to submit to, although, according to Avis Bunnage, she was initially disapproving. But Shelagh was a nineteen-year-old girl with no hands-on experience of the theatre at all. Despite her subsequent bravura performances in front of the world's press, she was the ultimate novice and when interviewed on the eve of the play's transfer to the West End she admitted: "in production, I think Joan Littlewood is the most valuable person I've ever met …"[10]

What was crystal-clear from the original script, however, was Delaney's firm grasp of dialogue, her ear for the cadences and rhythms of both everyday speech as well as that employed on the popular stage, the music hall in particular. Arthur Oberg, an American critic and academic, put his finger on this quality of the work when he said Delaney combined, "Lancashire vernacular with the 'bounce' of the music-hall line".

She joins the energy of the "once vital music-hall to the energy of speech-vocabulary, idiom, and syntax that is freshly colloquial in ways that middle and upper-class English speech is not. One hears in the play a conscious selection taken from the speech Shelagh Delaney spoke and heard from childhood. And one sees routines familiar to the playwright from popular entertainment."[11]

This latter aspect was clearly something that appealed immensely to Littlewood, who would continue to develop it until climaxing her own career with the exuberant quasi-musical extravaganza *Oh! What a Lovely War*. What Shelagh had given Littlewood to work with was a script that utilised all the techniques and tricks of classic comedy routines, the traditional comic 'business' found in music hall and variety, something Littlewood had noticed immediately when she remarked, "Then again, some of the dialogue sounded more like music-hall": and quoted,

| Helen: | Are you afraid of the dark? |
| Jo: | You know I'm afraid of the dark. |
| Helen: | You should try not to be afraid of the dark. |
| Jo: | I do try not to be afraid of the dark. |
| Helen: | And yet you're still afraid of the dark? |
| Jo: | I'm still afraid of the dark. |
| Helen: | Then you must try harder. |
| Jo: | I'll do that. |

For what would immediately capture audiences and reviewers alike, given the downbeat nature of the storyline, was how funny the play was when presented by Theatre Workshop. From the tabloids to the broadsheets, the words 'humorous', 'entertaining', 'lively', 'alive' peppered the reviews. Its shape, its lack of character development, its ambiguous meaning – these were noted and attributed in the main to Shelagh's 'apprentice' status; but what swept all before it was the sheer exuberance of the theatrical experience, what Kenneth Tynan described as the "joking and flaring and scuffling" of the characters and their "zest for life".[12]

*A Taste of Honey* constantly utilises both visual and verbal slapstick routines, employing a main comedy duo in Helen and Jo (Helen as the voluble, excitable one and Jo the sardonic, wisecracking one, constantly deflating Helen's extravagant statements.) They are joined later by Peter, a comedy 'spiv', to make a sparring threesome. The 'boy-girl act' of Jo and Jimmie is followed by another duo – Geof and Jo – who then combine with Peter and Helen.

There is the music-hall 'chase' ("Let me get hold of her," cries Helen, as Geof, trying to restrain her, appeals back and forth to the two of them: "Please Jo, Helen, Jo, please!"), while extra effect is achieved when Geof's temper breaks just as the two women pause for breath so that he is left yelling, "Will you stop shouting you two?" into complete silence. In the second act, Peter reappears as a 'slapstick drunk', falling over things, singing taglines from songs while hurling vivid insults at all and sundry.

Another traditional piece of stage business, the 'calamity', is regularly employed: drunken Peter "falls into the kitchen" where almost at once, "there is a loud crash." A similarly adroit use of off-stage noises occurs when Jo is in the kitchen trying to light the gas cooker. Helen's query, "Did you find it?" is followed by a "Loud bang", a pause, then Jo's rueful, understated response, "Yes."

A regular source of amusement is Jo's elaborate, droll put-downs of Helen's pretensions, as when she remarks, when Peter and Helen are thinking of buying an engagement ring , "I should have thought that their courtship had passed the stage of symbolism."

Helen, too, earns laughs when employing the unexpected, deflationary verbal anti-climax: "When I find somewhere for us to live I have to consider something far more important than your feelings [she pauses while we wonder what powerful and amazing motive this can be before adding]: The rent!" She also employs unexpectedly long and impressive words for a fairly ordinary meaning, as with, "The extent of my credulity always depends on the extent of my alcoholic intake."

While all this might appear somewhat artificial, it is complemented by Delaney's ability to capture the way people *actually talk*, particularly their tendency to jump from one subject to another in the middle of a speech (*Helen*: 'I said nobody asked you to come. Oh my God! I'll have to have a dose of something. My head's swimming. Why did you?').

There was also something else about the dialogue that Littlewood noticed: that Helen often seemed to be speaking to herself. Littlewood took things one step further, considering that it would make more 'theatrical sense' if she talked to the audience. Thus, from Helen's first direct address the audience became not just spectators but participants in the performance. Avis Bunnage, an experienced music-hall and revue performer as well as a straight actor was, according to Murray Melvin, the only one who was allowed to address the audience directly. Melvin later explained: "Avis could do it because she had the experience – she just did it so wonderfully. Joan would not let Frances Cuka or myself do it because we did not have enough experience to get away with it in any assured way."[13]

Not everyone appreciated this theatrical device. Reviewer Kenneth Tynan declared in the *Observer*: "I don't know that I like all of Miss Littlewood's production tricks: I don't see why the mother should address all her lines to the audience, like a vaudeville soloist."

Others saw the connection. The *Guardian*'s Philip Hope-Wallace wrote: "Avis Bunnage plays this feckless mother with a hard-faced good cheer which puts us in mind at once of that clever music-hall comic Hilda Mundy with perhaps a dash of Florence Desmond impersonating Gracie Fields."[14]

There are more academic ways of describing this technique, this breaching of the theatrical frame. According to Nadine Holdsworth, it was "a Brechtian-style alienating device that points up the artifice of theatrical practice".[15]

Though hard to believe today, the removal of this theatrical 'fourth wall' took audiences both at Stratford and later in the West End by complete surprise and simply added to the fun. It has also provided a score of veteran actresses playing the part down the years with opportunities to 'ham it up' completely.

Another development attributed to Littlewood's inspiration which would also make evenings at Stratford and later at theatres all round the world so lively when mounting the play was the addition of music – live music – to the production. Littlewood suggested in her autobiography that she hit on the idea of having a jazz band on stage because there was a need to link various scenes in the play that had no smooth way of being connected. This was because, in Delaney's play, there were few clearly marked scenes: action and situation tended to fade in and out rather like a sequence of snatched recollected dreams.

Johnnie Wallbank's Apex Trio jazz band – trumpet, guitar, drums and saxophone – was thus located on-stage and its music did more than just link scenes. Each character in the play was assigned a signature tune (music hall again) both to signify emotion and to attract audience empathy. ("John Bay ... underscored his part with snatches of popular song. On his first entrance, 'Getting to know you, getting to know all about you,' to Helen.")[16] The actors would regularly dance on and off stage with the aid of props, such as a broom or a tray of cups. The actors would even occasionally refer to the band and encourage them to "vamp it up".

The numbers played included, 'Careless Love', 'Dippermouth Blues' and 'Baby Doll', and to these Littlewood added Jo's song, an adaptation of, 'In the Pines', also known as 'Black Girl' and 'Where Did You Sleep

Last Night', a traditional American folk song dating back to the 1870s, though she adapted the lyrics from "Black girl, black girl, don't lie to me" to "Black, black boy, don't you lie to me."

Wallbank himself later explained, "We always opened the show with a very fast twelve-bar blues – it was never written down. The other bright tune we played was 'Everybody Loves My Baby' by Spencer Williams or sometimes we played 'I Found a New Baby' [also by Spencer Williams] – they're very similar harmonically. We'd change whenever we got bored of one, and nobody seemed to mind much whether we changed it or not."[17]

In addition to the jazz, Wallbank says, "there was some recorded music in it as well. When they come back from the fair, she's got a bunch of balloons and there's some sort of fairgroundy music, barrel-organ music sort of stuff just at the beginning of it."[18]

Using 'trad' jazz may not seem particularly radical today but in the 1950s jazz was associated with intellectuals, art school students, beatniks and Campaign for Nuclear Disarmament supporters. It signified subversion and rebellion both to those who enjoyed it and to those who abhorred it. It would later be used as a soundtrack to Ken Russell's *Monitor* film of Shelagh Delaney's Salford, while the original Angry Young Man in *Look Back in Anger*, Jimmy Porter, had played a jazz trumpet.

The music was credited with enticing younger audiences to the play, thus enlivening the proceedings. Littlewood later wrote: "Shelagh sat through the first run with music. She didn't utter a word. 'What do you make of it?' I asked her. 'I think it's going to be all right,' she said."[19]

Littlewood and others also later claimed that Shelagh had not noticed that difference between her first draft and the company's adaptation, but this is a little hard to believe. She was closely involved throughout in writing and rewriting sections as the play took shape, something she continued to do during its successful first run.

Shelagh certainly was correct about the play being 'all right'. Instead of proving to be Theatre Workshop's swansong, its subsequent success would play a major part in keeping the theatre open. Its initial two weeks were extended into a triumphant six-week run. Littlewood wrote: "The audience arrived along with agents and newshounds, anxious to get the low-down on this teenage wonder: Louis MacNeice, the poet, came, slightly abashed to find himself watching 'this adolescent effusion.'"[20]

In early June, the *Salford City Reporter* visited Shelagh at her home in Duchy Road to interview her. She explained that she was working on an amended version of the play which she had seen performed three times before returning home. The report continued: "Lounging in her favourite chair in slacks and a shirt, she said, 'I thought the group performed it very well but I am still trying to improve it in places ... They told me the attendances were pretty good the first week but I hardly noticed things from where I was in the balcony,' she confessed. She had travelled alone to the premiere: 'I couldn't bear to have any of my family with me.' Her mother seemed perturbed by some of the criticisms made of the play in the national press but Shelagh smiled and said that, 'they only made things more interesting.'"[21]

The play was soon attracting wider interest. Joan Littlewood noted, "*Honey* was doing so well that the vultures were appearing. Gerry was warned that George Devine of the Royal Court had advised Shelagh to drop Gerry and transfer Honey to his theatre. 'If the play is to transfer, I'd sooner it went to the West End than the Royal Court,' Gerry told him."[22]

Gerry Raffles would have his wish. Having been impressed with the play at Stratford, producer Oscar Lewenstein told Donald Albery, chairman and managing director of Wyndham Theatres Ltd, that he wanted to bring it to the West End. Albery went to see it and proposed they present it together. It was, according to Littlewood, the first time any West End manager had approached them – but she resisted the demand to recast the play with star names.

On 20th January 1959, *A Taste of Honey* was revived with the original cast at Stratford as a run-in for its transfer to the West End where it became a London hit and ran for almost a year, first at Wyndham's Theatre from 10th February 1959, and thereafter at the Criterion from 8th June.

Its transfer earned the Theatre Workshop company substantial funds, enough to enable it to put on *The Quare Fellow* by Brendan Behan, which would become another 'hit' transfer, establishing a profitable but, for Theatre Workshop an ultimately destructive trend. It would now regularly lose actors and writers, drawn to more profitable enterprises, and eventually find itself unable to continue as a viable operation.

Where Shelagh was concerned, however, a new world was opening up in a hurry and her life, both in London and particularly back home in Salford, would never be the same again.

NOTES

1 Littlewood, *Joan's Book*.
2 *Guardian*, 9th October 1990.
3 *SCR*, 20th June, front page: 'Play Writing' (Saul Reece).
4 Alec Patton, 'Jazz and Music-Hall Transgressions in Theatre Workshop's Production of A Taste of Honey', *New Theatre Quarterly*, 23, 4 (November 2007), pp. 331–6.
5 John Russell Taylor, *Anger and After*, 2nd edn (Methuen, 1969), p. 122.
6 Littlewood, *Joan's Book*.
7 Stephen Lacey, *British Realist Theatre: The New Wave in Its Context, 1956-1965* (Routledge, 1995).
8 Ibid.
9 *The 'Encore' Reader: A Chronicle of the New Drama*, ed. Tom Milne, Owen Hale and Charles Marowitz (Methuen, 1965), p. 230.
10 ITN News, 9th February 1959.
11 'A Taste of Honey and the Popular Play', reviewed by Arthur K. Oberg, *Wisconsin Studies in Contemporary Literature*, 7, 2 (Summer 1966), pp. 160–7.
12 *Observer*, 1st June 1958.
13 Murray Melvin to author.
14 *Guardian*, 11th February 1959.
15 Nadine Holdsworth, *Joan Littlewood's Theatre*, (Cambridge University Press, 2011).
16 Littlewood, *Joan's Book*.
17 Patton, 'Jazz and Music-Hall Transgressions'.
18 Ibid.
19 Littlewood, *Joan's Book*.
20 Ibid.
21 *SCR*, 6th June 1958, p. 4: 'Shelagh Has Right Idea'.
22 Littlewood, *Joan's Book*.

# 6

# 'The Smell of Living'

I went with Doycie to *A Taste of Honey,* a squalid little piece
about squalid and unattractive people. It has been written
by an angry young lady of nineteen and is a great success.
Personally I found it fairly dull.

Noël Coward, *Journals,* May 1959

*A Taste of Honey*'s box-office success wasn't always reflected in critical
comment. It would at first receive decidedly mixed reviews; whilst
conceding it possessed energy and humour, some critics slated its lack of
coherence and ramshackle construction.

W.A. Darlington writing, for the *New York Sunday Times,* suggested
that Delaney had little idea what to do with the characters she had
created. "Neither she nor they seemed to have any purpose. Each of them
pursued his or her uncharted course without reference to the others or
any but the most inconsiderable influence upon one another. There was
no continuity and no progress; the only individual concerned who
seemed to be making any headway was the baby ... "[1]

T.C. Worsley in the *New Statesman* felt that Joan Littlewood's
considerable input was crucial: "I feel that played perfectly straight it
would have been much too thin to hold the stage at all."[2]

The Arts Council drama panel, when awarding Shelagh a bursary of
between £100 and £150 soon after its Stratford premiere, felt moved to
comment that the play had been "reluctantly recommended because it
has a sort of strength in its crudity ... This is a good bad play. It seems
to have been dashed off in pencil in a school exercise book by a youngster
who knows practically nothing about the theatre and rather more about
life than she can at present digest ... Miss Delaney writes with the
confidence of sheer ignorance."[3]

On the other hand, the respected playwright and author Emlyn
Williams, when presenting Shelagh with a Charles Henry Foyle Award

in December 1958, declared that individuality, imagination and humour were what he looked for in a new playwright rather than the kind of "smooth construction you get in so many American plays by college-taught dramatists". Prophesying that she would become a "real major playwright" he said her first play was most touching and funny and the scene between boy and girl was "one of the most charming off-beat love scenes written for a very long time".[4]

It has been claimed that Kenneth Tynan's positive review in the *Observer* swung opinion round, just as his eulogy of *Look Back in Anger* back in 1956 had rescued and launched John Osborne's fledgling career. Tynan declared that Delaney was, "19, and a portent". He wrote, "There are plenty of crudities in Miss Delaney's play; there is also, more importantly, the smell of living … Miss Delaney brings real people onto her stage, joking and flaring and scuffling and eventually out of the zest for life she gives them, surviving. Suffering, she seems to say, need not be tragic; anguish need not be neurotic; we are all, especially if we come from Lancashire, indestructible."

Tynan was immensely influential; but he would not be the sole reason why *A Taste of Honey* became such an tremendous hit. Something about its nature and even the author herself attracted an intellectual, predominantly left-wing audience from the very beginning.

The *News Chronicle* reported that Tom Driberg, a left-wing MP, writer and journalist, after seeing the play on its first night, thought it, "enormously interesting and alive. It was a great pity the authoress didn't come on stage to take a bow at the end. She was too shy." Michael Foot, another left-wing politician and future Labour Party leader said, "Absolutely first class. We are very pleased Tom brought us along." Miss Delaney went back-stage where she met another member of the audience, Margot Fonteyn, who congratulated her. "A very exciting play indeed," she said.[5] Very soon, the play was being taken extremely seriously by a variety of contemporary commentators, and it is instructive to listen to what they had to say about it.

The England of 1958 is a distant land that few can now recall with any clarity. Back then, what Delaney and Littlewood had brought to the stage was something quite novel, particularly in terms of its treatment of marginalised characters. As the novelist and journalist Colin MacInnes put it: "*A Taste of Honey* … considers contemporary themes and characters unrepresented anywhere else: working-class child-mothers, ageing semi-professional whores, the authentic agonies of homosexual love, and the new race of English-born coloured boys …"[6]

There were some who looked upon the recipe with cynicism: T.C.Worsley, writing in the *New Statesman* in February 1959 was particularly scathing: "'Everyone' knows that her play is 'about' a tart, a black boy giving a white girl a baby, a queer. The whole contemporary lot, in short. And so 'everyone' will go expecting a play about tarting, queerness and miscegenation. But it won't take long to get around that the play isn't exactly 'about' any of these things; that we don't see Wolfenden women on the beat or Wolfenden boys on the game; that all the contemporary shock elements may be present but there's nothing very shocking to experience. And then the excitement may drop cruelly down."[7]

Others, however, saw things completely differently and considered the play genuinely ground-breaking in its wider social relevance. Questions of class were paramount. Colin MacInnes declared: "It is … the first play I can remember about working-class people that entirely escapes being a 'working-class play': no patronage, no dogma – just the thing as it is, taken straight." What's more, it "gives a great thirst for more authentic portraits of the mid-20th century English world. As one skips through contemporary novels, or scans the acreage of fish-and-chip dailies and the very square footage of the very predictable weeklies, as one blinks unbelievingly at 'British' films and stares boss-eyed at the frantic race against time that constitutes the telly, it is amazing – it really is – how very little one can learn about life in England here and now."[8]

Stuart Hall, cultural theorist and sociologist, writing in the *New Left Review,* agreed, considering the play "a rich, humane fragment drawing upon working class life. Shelagh Delaney has made authentic use of her Salford experience, with an honesty which makes even the current 'realism' of other plays seem frail by comparison," and he contrasted it with Osborne's work: "It is this note of human acceptance which gives the relationships between characters in the play their resonance, and which distinguishes *Taste of Honey* from the other plays, notably Osborne's, where the relationships are genuinely bitter, inward turned, corrosive."[9]

Lindsay Anderson, the film, theatre and documentary maker who would soon feature closely in Delaney's creative life, admitted: "Going north in Britain is always like a trip into another country, and *A Taste of Honey* is a real escape from the middlebrow, middle-class vacuum of the West End. It is real, contemporary poetry in the sense that its world is both the one we know and read about every Sunday in the *News of the World* – and at the same time the world seen through the eyes and imagination of a courageous, sensitive and outspoken person."[10]

Anderson felt that "the total commercialization, the deadening over-organization of the big societies of today make us prize more than ever the naive, spontaneous, honest visions of youth. This is where this play compares interestingly with *The Catcher in the Rye*. Like Holden, Josephine is a sophisticated innocent. Precious little surprises her; but her reactions are pure and direct, her intuitions are acute, and her eye is very sharp."

Critic, novelist and journalist Caryl Brahms wrote in *Plays and Players*: "Not, you will say, a pretty play. But a play which shines with the beauty of truth. A play which flashes with the grim wit that salty people pull out against themselves as mother and daughter claw verbally at one another ... A contemporary play dug out of the present minute, like its daffy heroine and the life that goes on all around her."[11]

One of the few extended analyses of the play, rather than a review, was produced by American academic John Parry, who picked up on Delaney's suggestion that she had written the play after seeing Rattigan's *Variation on a Theme* and thought she could do better. Placing her in the 'new group of dramatists' such as John Osborne, Arnold Wesker and John Arden, he felt the difference between them and the established writers such as Rattigan was that the latter had to keep within a strict moral 'respectable' code, not a code the real world would recognise but an 'official' as opposed to a 'private' set of rules. A dramatist like Delaney, on the other hand, was searching for a reality beneath the one accepted as reality, the "received official view". It wasn't immorality she was exploring, as she did not, "identify moral truth with the official standards of our present-day society". She was seeking something more intense, and "this alone puts her in a different category from the West End type of playwright producing scripts for the entertainment industry." What's more, it was the "attempt more than the achievement which distinguishes the artist from the hack". Hers was "a deep and passionate concern for human beings". She eschewed motivation, "or at least the sort of motivation that we have become accustomed to in the theatre: for this seems to them little more than a facile surface, a pat set of ideas and prejudices which tend more to hide than to illuminate the real person. Thus, Shelagh Delaney is rejecting the system of received values, just as she rejects the whole idea of a pattern in human events. Things just happen; they are not part of a grand design. If they do have any causes, these are likely to be small and unimportant, often accidental."[12]

In America itself, where the play would appear the following year, its perceived qualities of honesty, truth and humanity also struck a chord, although American reviewers were somewhat less taken by the apparent optimism amid the gloom detected by British critics. Shelagh, when interviewed about the play, had felt that the two women's lives produced not depression but resilience: "No one in my play despairs. Like the majority of people they take in their stride whatever happens to them and remain cheerful."[13]

The *New York Times*'s Howard Taubman noted that "the Lancashire lass may grow more optimistic as she grows older." Taubman did not see Delaney's pessimism as a deterrent, however, finding in her play, "the redeeming savor of truth", but Walter Kerr of the *New York Herald Tribune* thought that Delaney created interesting characters, from whom all "pretensions to dignity" had been removed. *A Taste of Honey*, he felt, "doesn't taste like honey, it tastes like vinegar spiced with ginger," while Robert Coleman of the *New York Mirror*, opining that a playwright should have "something important to say", referred to her as "a snarling, cynical young Englishwoman" who had written "an ode to misery".

Henry Popkin noted that Delaney's honesty had been, perhaps, a little too harsh for some: "The callousness of this little family had to be toned down for export. I think a simple national rule governs here: unless unusual national prejudices operate, it is only we who can believe the worst of our fellow countrymen; we can confidently paint in darkest colors the vices of those whom we know intimately. And so, Miss Delaney is unsparing in presenting her British characters whereupon the French and Americans throw up their hands and exclaim that no mother could be so unfeeling. In the Paris production, the mother was made a good old soul who does not expel the homosexual; in New York, as played by Angela Lansbury, she has some signs of kindness unknown to her London counterpart. The daughter, played here with great bounce and energy by Joan Plowright, is made a little less casual as she brings about her misfortunes."[14]

That alterations in the script would be made as it was translated and presented in various countries, as was soon happening to *A Taste of Honey*, was inevitable. However, it didn't go unnoticed that the play's transfer from Stratford East to the West End had seen some unusual, not to say unpleasant, changes in its content and tone. When the play premiered in New York, the prominent black magazine *Ebony*, beneath a headline 'Interracial Love Treated Frankly and Uncensored', noted that, "Jo's brief romance with the transient negro sailor actually occupies only a small portion of the play and, although portrayed with unabashed frankness, uncensored and passionate, it is … handled with taste and sympathy."

Ironically, it was the question of race that exercised one of the play's original champions, Stuart Hall, when he saw the production again in early 1959 at Wyndham's Theatre. There were, he suggested, "worrying changes in the script". In the original text, the final dialogue had proceeded thus:

| | |
|---|---|
| Jo: | Helen. |
| Helen: | Yes. |
| Jo: | Helen. My baby may be black. |
| Helen: | You mean that sailor was a negro? |
| Jo: | Yes. |
| Helen: | What was his name?" |
| Jo: | Jimmie. |
| Helen: | Yes. Then the father was Jimmie, then, wasn't it? |

Hall felt that the dialogue was "true to the way the relationships have been treated elsewhere in the play. The colour of the baby and Jo's lover is immaterial. Helen absorbs this, together with Jo's pregnancy, with an immediate, direct human acceptance of the facts ... For the first time in a recent play, the question of 'colour' is contained within the framework of the human values established for us on other, more authentic grounds."

However, the final lines had been changed for the West End. They now ran,

| | |
|---|---|
| Jo: | Helen. |
| Helen: | Yes? |
| Jo: | My baby may be black. |
| Helen: | You filthy bitch! |
| Jo: | I knew you'd say that ... Where are you going? |
| Helen: | To get myself a drink. Black! A picanniny! A bloody chocolate drop! Oh, my God! Can you see me wheeling a pram with a – I'll have to have a drink. |

Hall found the changes offensive, "not because of the actual lines Helen is made to speak, but because they seem to me to deny the spirit of the rest of the play. They do Helen a kind of violence which she nowhere deserves. They are gratuitous and arbitrary."[15]

Kenneth Tynan agreed: "I can't understand why the original ending, in which she accepted the Negro paternity of her daughter's baby, has been altered to permit her to make unattractive jokes about piccaninnies and 'bloody chocolate drops'."[16]

For Hall, the answer was clear enough. It was the "Scylla of the West End, and the Charybdis of success … Anything could happen, so long as the play remained at Stratford. It was untouchable. But once it hit Wyndham's, the machine of success went quickly into action. Anything is buyable: everyone is out for success."[17]

Joan Littlewood felt that not just the play had changed. "Shelagh now had a new typewriter – a gift from Graham Greene. She used it to type a letter to Gerry telling him that John Osborne (author of *Look Back in Anger*) and "some American" wanted her to meet them in New York, all expenses paid, and she wanted to go. Gerry couldn't forbid her, though he felt that she was young in the ways of the world and advised her to be wary. We heard no more."[18]

Some weeks later: "At the theatre, Shelagh was sitting in the vestibule waiting for Gerry. I'm going to buy that red sports car I've had my eye on," she told him.

"Who's going to drive it?" said Gerry. "In any case, your money is in the bank and will remain there till you're twenty-one." She said nothing but wrote him a note: *"I've never liked being told what to do and I've no intentions of starting to like it now. You have no right whatsoever to order me about like some Industrial Revolution employer. I'm not going to crawl round people's backsides like some suckholing spineless fly. I've been offered a lot of money for the film rights of my play and I want that car."*

"And that was that! As if we hadn't enough on our plate without trying to control Shelagh. All the same, Gerry managed to persuade her not to buy the car."[19]

NOTES
1   *New York Times*, 15th March 1959, p. 3.
2   *New Statesman*, 21st February 1959, pp. 253–4.
3   *Joan's Book*.
4   *SCR*, 12th December 1958, p. 7.
5   *News Chronicle*, 11th February 1959.
6   *Encounter* (April 1959), p. 70.
7   *New Statesman*, 21st February 1959, pp. 253–4.
8   *Encounter* (April 1959), p. 70.
9   Stuart Hall, 'Cultural Notebook: Taste of the Real Thing', *Universities & Left Review*, 6 (Spring 1959).
10  Lindsay Anderson, in *Encore* (July 1958).
11  Caryl Brahms, 'Salad Days in Darkest Salford', *Plays and Players* (April 1959).
12  John Parry, 'Morality and the New Drama', *Contemporary Review*, 202 (November 1962), p. 252.
13  Shelagh Delaney, *A Taste of Honey* (Heinemann, 1959).

14  'Theatre Chronicle', review by Henry Popkin, *The Sewanee Review*, 69, 2 (April–June 1961), pp. 333–45.
15  Stuart Hall 'Perils of the West End', *Universities & Left Review*, 6 (Spring 1959).
16  Source untraced.
17  Stuart Hall 'Perils of the West End'.
18  *Joan's Book*.
19  *Joan's Book*.

# 7

# Sweet Success

"Frankly, I'm fed up with being interviewed," confesses the New Playwright, as she lights up a small cigar. "They all ask me the same questions. If it isn't sex it's Françoise Sagan."

**Shelagh Delaney, *Daily Mail*, February 1959**

From the moment the play was scheduled to appear in the West End, Shelagh's profile was significantly raised. In the space of just six months she would emerge from complete obscurity to become a national celebrity. W.A. Darlington wrote in the *New York Times* that she "seemed likely to cause a sensation as startling as that which had swept London 150 years ago when Master Betty the boy tragedian was acclaimed a genius."[1]

Her face and figure, her love life and dress sense would all would be pored over as a composite picture, or rather a caricature, was built up: a cigar-smoking 'beatnik', hard-drinking, fast-car-mad Angry Young Woman.

It was clear to some that she was being promoted. As T.C. Worsley noted, "Miss Shelagh Delaney has every reason to be grateful to the publicity boys who have done a wonderful job for her – for the short run, which is all that publicity boys have to worry about."[2]

If not exactly promoted, her cause had been taken up by two media-wise men whose joint production company was expediting the play's transfer from Stratford to Wyndham's Theatre: Oscar Lewenstein and, in particular, Wolf Mankowitz.

Mankowitz was a man of many trades and talents and would play a large part in Delaney's creative life over the next couple of years. Born of Russian-Jewish descent in 1924 in Fashion Street, Spitalfields in the East End of London, he went to Cambridge, became a journalist and literary critic as well as a specialist in Wedgwood china which he bought and sold from an antiques shop in Piccadilly Arcade. At the same time he was writing short novels. *Make Me an Offer* appeared in 1952 and *A Kid for Two Farthings* a year later. Both became popular films. He then turned to the theatre and scored a considerable success with *The Bespoke Overcoat* (1953), an update of a Gogol short story.

In 1958 he wrote a musical, *Expresso Bongo*, based on the career of the pop star Tommy Steele, which was filmed the following year and was voted best British musical of the year in a Variety Annual Survey of shows on the London stage. In 1959, he was busy adapting *Make Me an Offer* as a stage production for the Theatre Workshop. Unlike Delaney, however, he successfully resisted the Littlewood improvisation process, and the piece soon transferred to the New Theatre, Oxford where it ran until 1960. Mankowitz also worked in television, writing two drama series for ATV in 1958, and hosting his own interview series, *Conflict*, also for ATV. With his contacts in the press and television, and his flair for publicity, it would be his guiding hand that would be behind the emergence of Delaney as the theatrical sensation of 1959.

She had started appearing in the newspapers as early as the New Year. Photos of her posing in a 'sloppy jo' sweater and slacks in front of the fire in Duchy Road appeared simultaneously on 2nd January[3] accompanied by the words "Spend, spend, spend" – a phrase that would become synonymous a year later with the doomed Viv Nicholson, another Northern lass suddenly replete with cash.

Shelagh, it was claimed by the *Daily Mail*, had signed a film deal worth £20,000 and would be earning another £200 a week from the play, money she was apparently anxious to spend on "A fast sports car with an open top. New clothes for brother Joe. Lots of holidays for Mum." She was reported as liking, 'boozing' – "beer, gin and lime, anything" – and wanting to travel. She had also written another play but it wasn't 'sordid': "I wish I hadn't got the sordid tag. I just write about things that really happen."[4]

The *Manchester Evening News* piece pictured her reclining in a chair in the same front room, looking glum beneath the headline, 'Shelagh Looks in Anger at Boyfriend Story'. The article mentioned the money she was earning once again but dwelt on an apparently erroneous report that she was planning to go on a world trip with a seventeen-year-old boy called Jim Proctor. Shelagh said, "I have never been out with Jim Proctor and he is certainly not going on a world trip with me." And then, confusingly, she added, "But it may be that I am in love with him, I don't know. Any talk about our getting married is stupid."[5]

There were, at this time, rather more serious rumours concerning herself and Irish playwright Brendan Behan. "We are both creatures of Joan's imagination," Behan once said, referring to his and Delaney's concomitant rise in the Theatre Workshop stable. Perhaps the suspected liaison between himself and Delaney was also imagination on the part of Fleet Street's columnists although Behan did seem to follow Delaney around at odd times. In mid-1961, with Shelagh busy at home in Salford trying to form a community theatre, the telephone rang. It was Behan speaking from New York and telling Shelagh that he was flying from the States to London en route to Manchester. As the local Salford newspaper reported, "When he reached our neighbouring city he paid a nice compliment to the young Salford writer: 'Manchester is an artistic wilderness so it is only right that I should call on its only flower.'"[6]

At least one of Behan's biographers is convinced there was something in the story. "Delaney's interest in Behan was not lost on Beatrice [Behan's wife], an artist and fellow Dubliner who took marriage seriously. She was not about to let her marriage founder over the affections of a girl scarcely out of her teens. In a brief exchange Beatrice told Delaney to cease and desist – if she wanted Brendan she would have to take him warts and all. The rumour soon faded and in any case Behan was to find himself with bigger distractions …"[7]

Her love life in general would be a recurring theme in interviews over the next few weeks, that and the 'sordid' nature of her play. However, she proved more than adept at coping with such queries, as her appearance on the ITN News on the eve of the play's opening would demonstrate.

The interviewer, speaking with cut-glass Received Pronunciation, starts: "Miss Delaney, you must be very excited about tonight. Have you got butterflies?" to which she replies, "No, I've just got a very bad cold, that's all that's worrying me …"

He continues, "It's rather a sordid theme. Where did you get your information?", to which, while giving him a quizzical smile and glancing cheekily at the camera, she retorts, "I just applied me imagination to me observation."

"Observation where – in your native Lancashire?"

"Well yes, it had to be there, I've never been anywhere else."

"I understand you're getting married soon?"

[Double take to camera as Shelagh declares, as if outraged]: "I'm not getting married soon at all! No!"

"It's been reported."

"It has been, yes, you know, but that sort of thing isn't usually very reliable is it?" [little laugh].[8]

There was a sense that she clearly enjoyed all the attention while at the same time appearing to be just slightly world-weary, and not a little cynical. Joan Littlewood commented: "Shelagh took it all in her stride, giving interviews, considering offers, opening her first bank account … She was seen in the right pubs coping with the latest drinks and entertaining her hosts with laconic comments in her broad Salford accent. 'Carefully cultivated,' said a London admirer."[9]

As the play opened in the first week of February, however, she appeared on television in a documentary feature that would define the way in which she would be reported thenceforth.

The late 1950s had seen the first flowering of independent television capturing enormous audiences and dwarfing for a time the once omnipotent BBC. 'Vox pop' programmes involving ordinary people and their opinions were an important part of the new schedules and Daniel Farson, originally a print journalist and photographer, specialised in seeking out the 'off-beat', the quirky and the unusual and bringing them to television's silver screen. During the late 1950s and early 1960s Farson made a series of programmes for the independent TV company Associated-Rediffusion, typical of them being *Out of Step*, showcasing people and subjects that seemed not to belong in the strict societal norms of the time. Other programmes included *Down with Work, Muscle Men, Anarchy, Down with Marriage* and *Witchcraft*. Farson was, as he himself put it, an "unlikely contemporary idol, but the power of television made me so".[10]

His series, *Success Story*, starting in February 1959 was another typical Farson project in which he set out to examine the "curious quality of success" by interviewing a group of 'successful' personalities, Shelagh Delaney amongst them.

It was an eclectic assortment including Lady Lewisham (otherwise known as Raine Legge, daughter of Barbara Cartland, whose stepdaughter was Princess Diana), Western pulp writer Hank Janson, the veteran politician Herbert Morrison, celebrity cooking couple Johnny and Fanny Craddock, restaurateur Charles Forte, clairvoyant Maurice Woodruff, even Hyperion, a British Derby-winning horse!

Shelagh Delaney's episode was filmed (perhaps inevitably) in her mother's front room in Duchy Road, Salford, with herself and Farson sitting on a rug in front of the fire. Oddly enough, it had been two features by Farson in the *Daily Mail* in July 1956 which had announced the emergence of a 'post-war generation' in literature, and which held

John Osborne, Colin Wilson, Michael Hastings and Kingsley Amis to be the representatives of a new literary movement. The media's interest in these 'Angry Young Men' as a group can be traced to Farson's articles; here he was interviewing the first 'Angry Young Woman'.

The *Daily Mail* ran a review of the episode beneath the headline, 'Shelagh Gives Us a Taste of Anger', declaring that "The Angry Young Woman took a swipe at the Angry Young Man on television last night." She had apparently scoffed at the idea of being an Angry Young Woman: "Anybody under the age of 30 is an angry young man or woman to people over 40 who once thought they might do something and never did," she said. Farson had then asked her if she'd seen *Look Back in Anger*.

"She replied, 'I saw it on television.' 'What did you think of it?' Shelagh, hesitating, threw back her tousled head and said guardedly in a broad Lancashire accent, 'I think I must have seen a bad production.'"[11]

According to Derek Hill, reviewing the series for *Sight & Sound*, Farson normally dominated those he interviewed and Hill decried what he called the "nervous attempts to make such material 'visual'", particularly the Hank Jansen episode where the writer was flanked by a masked figure in a Soho bar and the programme intercut with striptease dancers. It was "a supremely lunatic case in point". The Delaney episode, however, was television at its best, Delaney coming across as a natural screen personality.[12]

Tom Driberg, writing in the *New Statesman*, agreed. "After the glossiness of the shows (What's My Line?) in which reliable old pros are endemic, it is a welcome shock to encounter a natural 'natural'. Such was Shelagh Delaney in *Success Story*; she answered Dan Farson's questions (repetitive and below his usual high standard) with Lancashire aplomb and with cool ingratitude to her fan John Osborne, whose *Look Back in Anger* she described as 'bloody awful, as a whole'."[13]

The programme went out twice, once in the North and a few days later across the rest of the ITV regions. Coinciding with the triumph of her West End début, it catapulted Shelagh into the nation's living-rooms in a way that would be impossible today, setting the tone for the newspaper headline cacophony that followed: 'Shelagh of Salford Sips the Sweet Honey of Success (*Daily Express*); 'Shelagh Tastes Sweet Success' (*Daily Herald*); 'Miss Success Celebrates with a 7d Cigar' (*Daily Sketch*).

The play itself was greeted by the popular broadsheets with what were becoming almost clichés: "salty, down-to-earth"; "uncompromising to gasping point at times, as alive as the Saturday night streets of Salford"; "unsentimental and refreshing as a cold bath"; "uncommonly alive and kicking with a blend of maturity and immaturity (not to mention maternity) of penny dreadful and comic strip, down-to-earth slum drama, and airy slapstick, alternating glib cross-talk with moments of sheer poetry."

When criticism did occur, Shelagh would find herself with some weighty champions, in particular John Osborne, who wrote to the *News Chronicle*[14] complaining of the "snobbish" attitude of its theatre critic, Alan Dent, who'd complained about the "kitchen-sink" nature of the piece and the tendency for modern playwrights to "grovel and revel in dirt and decay". ("It is the latest example of the Lavatory School of drama which I am never going to enjoy as long as it doesn't want to come out of the lavatory ... Will the baby be black or pink or tangerine? I cannot be made to care and Miss Delaney will have to acquire much more dramatic skill be fore she can make me care.")

Osborne weighed in beneath a headline 'A Taste of Vinegar – from John Osborne': "The air of patronage and insensitivity of the notice of Shelagh Delaney's play which appeared in your newspaper is remarkable even for your critic." Suggesting that Dent had a "bigoted" image of Britain, "derived from the ages of daily newspapers, Jane Austen and glossy magazines devoted to gun dogs at point-to-point meetings", he concluded that it was "entirely predictable that he should be incapable of assimilating the human values of *Taste of Honey*", which was, "an acutely sensitive play about a group of warm, immediately recognisable people".[15]

However, for now the play was really not the thing. Shelagh herself was the object of attention along with the (to the national press at least) curious nature of her family and friends who were sharing her moment of fame:

"43-year-old Mrs Elsie Delaney, a bus-driver's widow, had come down to London to taste the honey of her daughter's success. 'Success is not going to change any of the family though,' she said (in broad Lancashire tones which clanged strangely above London's fashionable theatre-going voices.) She went on roundly, 'I've read Shelagh's play. It's sexy, but I don't think it's vulgar.' Shelagh Delaney smiled in the background and looked down at her silver slippers."[16]

"It was a great night for the Delaneys. They crowded into the back of the stalls – Uncle James and Aunt Mavis (who arrived just before curtain up because the cabbie had taken them to the Windmill by mistake ... 'Couldn't understand my accent, I suppose,' she said) and cousins Joan,

Tony and Freda Barry."[17]

Meanwhile, "Shelagh's brother Joe, a 17-year-old apprentice instrument maker, had brought his fiancée Anne Mulhull down to London (taking time off from the Salford knitwear factory where she earns £5 a week). And Shelagh's boyfriend? Why wasn't he there to see her in her silver slippers and the blush of her success? S said, 'I have a number of boyfriends. Some I've met in London.'"[18]

"Shelagh's mother, 43-year-old Mrs Elsie Delaney, a widow who lives in a 30s Salford council flat, bought a modest ten-guineas off-the-peg tweed suit for the occasion. 'I didn't want to pay a lot of money for something tailor-made,' she said."

The after-the-show dinner was held at the Talk of the Town restaurant. "She [Shelagh Delaney] came off the dance floor after dancing with her brother Joe and told me: 'We're all having a smashing time and everyone around me is from Salford.' One of her school chums said, 'Oooh look! There's a girl who was on Dotto [A popular TV quiz-show] the other night.' Said Shelagh, 'Oh you see everyone around here. The famous and the infamous.' But to me she confided, 'This is the first time I've been here.'"[19]

In fact, Delaney made various attempts to sabotage the sense of innocent glee: "Shelagh Delaney after eight curtain calls, puffed on a small cigar and wiped the sweat from her brow with the back of her hand. 'It's all been wonderful,' she said, 'in a nauseating sort of way.'"

It would, of course, be easy to identify what today would qualify as crude sexism permeating the reports: from describing Shelagh as "like a kennel-maid on her day off" (*News Chronicle*) to observing her as, "lumbering through the grey, wastes of Stratford, E15 in windcheater and jeans", easily mistaken for Bernard Bresslaw (a popular very tall TV comedian). There was almost an obsession with her size and dress-sense. Shelagh, naturally honest and forthright, offered plenty of artless quotes: "In close-up, however, hungrily wolfing down a meal of sausage, cabbage, beetroot, and weak tea at the local caff, the New Playwright is clearly female … 'I've always fancied myself as a blonde instead of a brunette. Still do. No, that's not true. I'd rather be a red-head now. I've had a go with a bottle every now and again but it's not much use to me. It's not that I want to be more attractive to men, no, I seem to manage alright as I am, thanks very much.'"[20]

The following day she allowed herself to be followed around London by the *Daily Express* and a photonews spread appeared showing her shopping for cigars, eating a pub lunch, reading the reviews and gazing out in Little Venice.

"Then to a car-showroom where gleams a dream of dreams that she has been eyeing for a week: a 1959 Chevrolet Corvette sports, top speed 150 mph price £3,734. 'I'm going to buy this one later. Three and a half weeks on Broadway and I'll have made it!' Salford had better watch out."[21]

Unfortunately, Salford needed no warning.

NOTES

1  *New York Times*, 15th March 1959. The famous Irish child actor William Henry West Betty (popularly known as 'Master Betty'), took the British Isles by storm in the early 19th century. Betty's first appearance at the Theatre Royal, Dublin, in 1803 was so much anticipated that the city authorities were forced to extend curfew by an hour to accommodate those attending. In London, there were even proposals to make him a ward of Chancery to protect him from the dangers of Bettymania. Betty's career stalled when he took time off to go to university. After a number of unsuccessful comebacks, he settled down to a quiet life of peace and good works on his very considerable savings, dying largely unremembered seventy years later.

2  *New Statesman*, 'The Sweet Smell', 21st February 1959, pp. 253–4.

3  *Daily Mail* and *Manchester Evening News*. 2nd January. The *Mail*'s headline, 'Shelagh's Taste of Money'.

4  *Daily Mail*, 2nd January 1959.

5  *Manchester Evening News*, 2nd January 1959.

6  *Salford City Reporter*, 11 August 1961.

7  Frank Gray, *The Crazy Life of Brendan Behan: The Rise and Fall of Dublin's Laughing Boy* (AuthorHouse, 2010).

8  ITN News.

9  *Joan's Book*.

10  Daniel Farson, *Never a Normal Man: An Autobiography* (HarperCollins, 1998).

11  *Daily Mail*, 9th February 1959.

12  Derek Hill 'Topical Television, Sight and Sound', *Film Quarterly*, 28, 2 (Spring 1959), p. 95.

13  Tom Driberg 'Pre-Frontal Personality', *New Statesman*, 21st February 1959, pp. 253–4.

14  *News Chronicle*, 13th February 1959.

15  *News Chronicle*, 14th February 1959.

16  *Daily Express*, William Hickey column, 11th February 1959.

17  *Evening News*, John Carpenter column, 11th February 1959.

18  *Daily Express*, William Hickey column, 11th February 1959.

19  *Daily Herald*, "A Honey of a Play by the Ex-usherette", 12th February 1959.

20  *Daily Mail*, The Robert Muller interview, 9th February 1959.

21  *Daily Express*, 12th February 1959.

# 8

# Salford Shocked

Her play, she said, had caused "a great divide" back home in
Salford. "Half the town says it's disgusting that I should
degrade it. The other half have got the sense to see that I am
not particularly degrading anybody. I'm just a writing a play."

**Shelagh Delaney, *New York Times*, March 1961**

That things were not going as well back home as they were in London
started to become evident as early as December 1958 when news of
Shelagh's good fortune reached Salford. In accepting the Charles Henry
Foyle Award she claimed that she had tried the 11+ exam four times,
"failing miserably on each occasion".

The *Salford City Reporter* ran an article on the front page headlined,
'Shelagh Delaney Accused of Ingratitude to her Teachers', with the
Director of Education, Mr F.A.J. Rivett quoted as saying, "The implied
sneer at the eleven-plus and the city's educational system is unfair and
unworthy ..."[1] Rivett then recounted her progress, suggesting that "had
she stayed on [at school] there is no doubt whatever that she could have
proceeded to university." He added that her desire to present herself as "a
native genius" who succeeded in the face of "a complete lack of
recognition is a form of inverted snobbery popular in certain circles in
London".[2] Pendleton High School, he concluded, deserved some credit.
Though he later wrote to claim that not all the observations attributed to
him were "made by me personally and, I think, are largely your own
editorial opinions", the tone of subsequent reports concerning Shelagh
had been set.

In January 1959 further details of her financial windfall were reported
and the accusation that she had been "decrying of her educational
benefits in the city", was repeated. But it was when the play first appeared
in print that the onslaught began in earnest. Saul Reece, the newspaper's
editor, had already expressed a certain scepticism concerning her claim

to have written the play in two weeks: "Nobody, no matter how experienced, skilled and competent can possibly dash off a real play in a couple of weeks."[3] It was, he asserted, a 'sketch' and she was 'lucky' to have sent it to Theatre Workshop who pulled off some "hair-raising stunts" to make it a success.[4]

At this point, it will be instructive to explain a little about Reece, as he was crucial in orchestrating the local reaction to Delaney's emergence as a national literary figure. Born in Lower Broughton, Salford in 1903, Reece was educated at Cheetham elementary school and after earning several scholarships managed to gain entry to Manchester Grammar School, and thence on to Manchester University.

A man of various talents, for some years he was a professional pianist but moved into journalism during the Second World War, working on smaller Manchester papers before joining the *Salford City Reporter*. He became its editor in 1949 and would remain so for almost 20 years. Associated with a number of welfare and social services in the Jewish community and appointed JP in 1962, he was very much a local man; his wife was also born in Salford and was associated with the Women's Zionist Association and worked for the Jewish Blind Homes. A son worked as a local Salford doctor; a daughter-in-law was a local midwife. He was, in fact, a pillar of Salford society.

The paper he edited, the *Salford City Reporter*, was a weekly broadsheet that appeared each Friday. In many ways a typical local paper, it covered the usual round of births, weddings and sports events, reviewed plays and films and gave full-page coverage to local events such as Carnival Queen elections, Whit Walks, and any celebrity appearances in the city such as *Coronation Street* stars opening shops or presenting prizes. It gave extensive coverage to the Magistrates' courts and, like many of its peers around the country, reported in full on any salacious rape or incest cases, national murder trials and robberies. It also ran extensive local history pieces and, as such, reflected a deep-seated pride in the city's past. Reece's 'Salford Scene' column in the *Salford City Reporter* was very much his own territory where he "highlighted the rights and wrongs of the handling of city affairs as seem by him". As a weekly, it was not as influential as the *Manchester Evening News*, for instance, but it was taken by the majority of Salfordians and was Salford's voice to the rest of the world.

A few weeks after calling into question Delaney's authorship of *A Taste of Honey*, Reece returned to the topic on 25th July 1958 when discussing another playwright who, "for the information of a certain young lady ... does not dash off his plays by inspiration in the interval

SHELAGH'S TASTE OF MONEY

By Daily Mail Reporter

SPEND, spend, spend. Quickly, too. A fast sports car with an open top. New clothes for mother Joe. Lots of holidays for Mum. Those are the New Year resolutions of the year-old S H E L A G H Delaney, the factory girl who won £152,319 British Premium...

SHELAGH—"Smart clothes? I'm killed in them"

Photo above: ©Mirrorpix

Photos below: ©Daily Herald Archive/
Science & Society Picture Library

*Top left:* "Spend, Spend, Spend.", 2nd January 1959 (*Daily Mail*).
*Top right:* At her first typewriter (*Daily Mirror*).
*Bottom left:* Selecting a disc in January 1959 (*Daily Herald*).
*Bottom right:* Home with dog Micky on her 21st birthday in November 1959 (*Daily Herald*).

**In the first year of her sudden rise to fame, Shelagh opened her house in Duchy Road to the national press with varying degrees of success.**

between tea and supper but served a hard apprenticeship as drama critic on a famous Midlands newspaper".[5] There was clearly something about Delaney that irked Reece.

Now, on 23rd January 1959, beneath a headline 'A Taste of Honey Has a Bitter Flavour', he dubbed the play 'a sordid tale,' continuing:

> As a fellow Salfordian pathetically keen to see Salford and its residents gain added fame, I should love dearly to go with the critics but alas my vote must be with the 'Noes' … I am happy to congratulate Miss Delaney on her success but, with all sincerity, must confess my amazement at the favourable impression *A Taste of Honey* has made. I have seen far better plays missing any favourable notice on their heart-breaking rounds of the third-class theatres. But if this is typical of the writings of our 'Angry Young Men' and 'Talented Young Women' I thank heaven that I am a small town square who still prefers J.B. Priestley and Emlyn Williams.[6]

When the play reached the West End, the paper's criticism grew harsher. On 13th February beneath the headline, 'A Taste of Cash for Shelagh But a Kick in the Teeth for Salford', a Dr Murray Reece criticised Delaney for the money she was about to make, ostensibly for denigrating her home town. "Alas poor Salford that the only emotion she arouses in the hearts of her talented sons and daughters is the desire to wipe their muddy boots on her! Until Tuesday such Londoners as knew of Salford thought of her as a *Love on the Dole* conglomeration of dirty slums inhabited by gin-swilling witches and lecherous bookies; since Tuesday they think of it as a place where girls of around nineteen are sufficiently informed on the subject of 'half-wits, half-castes, half-tarts, half-pimps and half-homosexuals' to write about them with ease and confidence."[7]

He'd never heard dialogue like it anywhere other than in a magistrate's court in cases involving "slummy neighbours", and expressed wonderment at the fact that a "mere 19 year old girl" could have known so much about the sordid facts of life, especially "an insight into the changing feelings of a pregnant mother". The only reason, he surmised, that the play had been accepted was because it would make everyone money, and he ended by asserting that the theatre critics hadn't really liked the play but were pulling their punches because they sensed it would be a hit!

Various readers of the *Reporter* were puzzled at the time as to exactly who Dr Murray Reece was. In fact, he was the editor's son and not a journalist at all. A technical executive with a multinational American corporation, he lived in London where his wife was a teacher with London

County Council. One can only presume that he was closer at hand to the West End than his father and thus was asked to write a review.

The following week, somewhat inevitably, the *Salford Reporter*'s postbag was said to be "colossal", led by Shelagh's own mother whose letter was posted on the front page of the paper beneath the headline, 'Mrs Delaney Says "Shelagh Loves Salford"'.[8] She expressed surprise at Reece's apparent lack of knowledge of the reality of day-to-day life: "Has he never seen slums or a white girl with a coloured baby? Has he never heard of sex?" Attacking the paper for its tendency to fill its pages with "Magistrates Courts' reports and scandal", she ended, "he had better be very careful what he says about my daughter, Miss Shelagh Delaney, or he will find himself in serious trouble."[9]

The readers' letters printed inside were largely against the play, although few if any of those writing in could have actually seen it! "Just a nasty piece of sordid filth which would not have arched an eyebrow had it been scripted for the sort of X film some French producers churn out with far less vulgarity."[10] "… a British girl spawning a literary monstrosity that bawled vilely as it crawled in the squalor its creator had libellously conceived to be typically Salfordian."[11] "No civic pride in writers, nothing to reflect the struggle out of poverty and degradation that the city is undergoing …"[12] "An execrable play which happens to contain the current jack-pot ingredients – vulgarity, perversion, lust, drink, abuse, squalor. It is not a book; it is not even a well-written play."[13]

One writer complained at "having to respond to people who say to him 'Oh you are from Piccaninny Town eh?' or 'So you are a Honey Bee'"; another woman claimed, "It will be the making of her. It will be the breaking of Salford …"; and an ex-musical director of Theatre Workshop, after naming most of those involved in the production, concluded, "All these people have lost their roots in the north and are now part of the 'conspiracy' of Londoners to treat Salfordians and other northerners as a lot of numbskulls."[14]

Not everyone was as scathing. One woman suggested Reece should "take a tour of Salford's day nurseries", if he was so shocked at real life. Jesse Hargreaves, the mother of Christine, a *Coronation Street* actress and one of Shelagh's best friends, wrote to say that she'd actually seen the play and liked it and that Shelagh had not intended to "kick Salford in the pants". She was, Mrs Hargreaves stated, a playwright and she'd used the materials at hand. She also suggested that some of the Reeces' comments "are close to libellous".[15] She later wrote to the *Manchester Evening News*, taking Salford's mayor to task for opining that the play was not fair to

Salford: "When are they going to open their eyes and admit that prostitution and squalor exist in Salford – and other parts of the country?"[16]

The following week, there were yet more letters including a long one from one Gerald Hodcraft in defence of Delaney headed 'Salford Can Be Proud of This Achievement' and citing Harold Hobson the drama critic and author on the BBC *Critics* programme, who had thought Delaney, "a dramatist born not one manufactured by study". Hodcraft said he was "appalled, even disgusted by the hysterical outbursts from certain Salfordians" who were either thin-skinned or lacking in intelligence. Yvonne Carter, of Brindle Heath Road, Pendleton wrote, "As a mere woman I find it hard to believe that a man with such an illustrious titles as 'Dr' Reece could really be as childish as he sounds …" Perhaps, she suggested, he would like a tour of Salford's day nurseries.[17]

News of the furore soon reached London and Wyndham's Theatre. In April, producer Donald Albery decided to write to Salford's mayor, "to invite you and any member of your corporation you may care to bring to be my guest in London to see a performance of *A Taste of Honey*. I feel that an unsympathetic view was taken by the Manchester press to the play and perhaps you have been given a wrong conception of the play …"[18] Whether the offer was taken up or not is unknown.

Even given Shelagh's overtly brash and super-confident demeanour, the home-town reaction came as something of a shock. She was only twenty years old and had been in the public eye for less than six months, yet she was being vilified in print, accused of exploiting her home town for cash, her talents and achievement openly queried. She remained defiant, however. When a *Salford Reporter* journalist caught up with her at Easter as she waited for a train to London he found her "unrepentant and very much matured".

"We had quite an interesting conversation about her play and the reaction it had caused here in Salford. Shelagh was obviously not the least bit worried about any sort of criticism. When I referred to the voluminous correspondence which we had received containing viewpoints both for and against the play Shelagh said her mother had sent her copies of the paper in which the letters appeared and told me, 'I could have laughed when I read some of them. The narrow provincial minds of some of these people amaze me. With great indignation they say that this sort of thing could not happen in Salford and in the same issue of the *Reporter* there appeared a court story of a woman who had allowed her house where her four children lived to be used as a brothel!'

Her parting shot was, 'If any of your readers thought my last play was shocking, wait until they see the next one!'"[19]

Six months later, relations between Shelagh and her local paper remained strained. "Salford's phenomenal young playwright is still very, very annoyed with us," wrote a reporter. Calling on her to seek her views to "congratulate her and ask her about her plans", the same reporter could only get as far as the doorstep of Duchy Road and Shelagh's comments were even more dismissive.

"I feel that the *Reporter* has been most unfair to me, and not only the *Reporter*, but others in Salford, too. People from Salford who have seen the play like it. It is unfair to condemn it without seeing it, and it's wrong to say I intended reflecting life in Salford. It could be anywhere. Even so there are stories in the *Reporter* – notably of incest – which are far worse than anything I portrayed in *Taste of Honey*." She concluded, "The *Salford City Reporter* is not fulfilling its duty as a weekly paper and it is only fit for what it is doing anyway – serving as a wrapper for fish and chips. But in any case, I'm not interested in the *Reporter*."[20]

Unfortunately, the paper remained interested in her and continued fanning the flames of criticism whenever possible. On 5th February it reacted with scorn to a request from the Bristol Old Vic, which was mounting a production of *A Taste of Honey*, for photos of some "poorer living conditions" in Salford, presumably for the play's programme. Such sniping was beginning to have its effect.

When the City Art Gallery asked Delaney if it could have the original script for *A Taste of Honey* she responded that she'd already given it to Theatre Workshop and "expressed her surprise that the Council should want the manuscript of a play about which so many of them were rude".[21] The *Salford Reporter*'s editor, beneath a headline 'Something Nasty', agreed – why would Salford wish officially to enshrine a document which has given a nationwide impression that Salford people are "a very odd lot"?[22]

This was too much for a group of local authority-employed builders, the Salford Direct Workers, who wrote from their Barracks site a letter defending her: "We should be proud of Shelagh" etc., and attacking the newspaper.

On behalf of the undersigned building workers I have been asked to come to the defence of Miss Shelagh Delaney on the basis that at the very least that it's about time somebody attempted to present a reasonable argument in what we believe is the deliberately manufactured controversy about this young Salford lass who has managed to achieve fame as a playwright.

Salford should surely be proud that it has produced a person who is achieving world-wide fame as a writer. We are usually noted for having the worst slums, the highest proportion of people suffering from various diseases and other things unmentionable perhaps in a play about people ...

Shelagh's crimes appear to be that she has "given a nationwide impression that Salford people are an odd lot" and that her way of speech is "common" ...

The very idea that Shelagh Delaney has cast a slur on Salford is absurd. It arises from a silly, parochial, narrow-mindedness that no citizen of any city should tolerate. As for Miss Delaney's speech, we, the undersigned, have had the pleasure of meeting her and we found that her speech was common, common that is to Salford folk, no airs and graces, no affectation, no "ectuallys" or "rather".[23]

Unfortunately, their arguments were falling on stony ground. It's perhaps very easy from the distance of over half a century to feel superior to Delaney's detractors and indignant at their apparently ridiculous and reactionary criticisms of both herself and her play.

Delaney saw herself writing a piece that extolled the virtues of the downtrodden and the marginalised. Her champions on the London cultural scene agreed, and saw something in *A Taste of Honey* that was liberating the theatre, first and foremost, from the stultifying grip of middle-class manners and light entertainment. Most of them were middle-class, university-educated and fighting left-leaning battles of their own, seeking to widen the struggle for control of channels of communication, seeking to reform what they felt were restrictive practices of the then governing classes: censorship, laws concerning sexual behaviour. Theatre was just one vehicle in that struggle. Shelagh might have thought she was just writing a play but for the London intelligentsia she was striking a blow for social freedom.

Salford might not be expected to appreciate that particular point of view. Its civic worthies were fighting more immediate battles: striving to deal with widespread, deep-seated poverty and deprivation amid the crumbling fabric of a city striving to enter the 20th century. The city felt uneasy, threatened by Manchester's looming presence.

Thus *A Taste of Honey* seemed to many such people not a liberating gust of fresh air, but rather a tasteless exhibition of lower-class seediness and immorality without any redeeming features whatsoever. Like Delaney herself, it seemed merely unrepentant and provocative. On top of that, and in common with much of the country north of Watford, Salford people resented being caricatured.

*Love on the Dole* by the local author Walter Greenwood, although written a quarter of a century earlier, still divided opinion. The book/play (and eventual film) had, it's true, been used during the war to galvanise those who wished to reform society and eradicate unemployment and its attendant vices. It had struck a sympathetic chord throughout the land. Yet still there remained a definite feeling that it painted a condescending, not to say patronising picture of Northern folk. Delaney herself had referred to her own unhappiness at the way in which people from the North were depicted as 'gormless' in literature and on screen. Whether she was referring to *Love on the Dole* is uncertain, for she never cited the play in interviews and would appear not to have met Walter Greenwood (presumably because, once well-off enough, Greenwood had chosen to live as far away from the city as possible, a fact often mentioned by his detractors).

The recent advent of television as a mass entertainment vehicle only served to accentuate the problem she posed. The nation might not have seen *A Taste of Honey* but it had seen and heard Shelagh. In the days when there were only two major TV channels, for a period in early 1959 there was no escape from her. Had she been male, things might have been different but there was clearly something about her manner, not to say her gender, that rubbed people up the wrong way.

The casual sexism of the national newspapers was mirrored in Salford, but in more traditional forms. One letter-writer had said that Delaney, "should have accepted her fame, 'with the grace and modesty of Judy Grinham, Pat Smythe, and the many others of her sex who have risen to the top of their talents'". Then perhaps her "cruel libel" of Salford would have been less unbearable.[24]

This was a city where, in common with other Northern industrial towns, soon-to-be brides were dressed up in ragged motley by their fellow female workmates and given a public send-off at the factory gate: pictures of such light-hearted events regularly graced the pages of the *Salford Reporter*. The city also ran a much-heralded beauty competition each year and the *Reporter* trailed the search for contestants for months prior to the big day. Miss Salford Carnival Queen truly represented what Salford considered to be the ideal young woman. Generally well turned out, she was usually on the cusp of marriage, had probably stayed on at school for a year or two to gain qualifications as a secretary or a teacher – and she thought Salford a wonderful place.

Shelagh had eschewed almost every one of those attributes/pathways. In conventional terms, she wasn't attractive and seemed intent on presenting herself in such a way as accentuated her oddness: smoking cigars, wearing what appeared to be shabby clothes in public, drinking to excess. The insouciant eleven-year-old girl from *Sweetly Sings the Donkey*, who had teased and infuriated the nuns in her convalescent home with her cheeky back-chat and sly teasing, had metamorphosed into her equally obnoxious and irritating elder sister. What's more, to the casual onlooker, she appeared not to have worked too hard to achieve success. She had dropped out of education at the first opportunity, had omitted to thank her hard-working teachers and had tumbled into a new and rich world in the South where she was happy to spend her money in what might be termed vulgar pursuits: fast cars, drink and glamorous holidays. For those who termed themselves respectable, Shelagh ticked all the wrong boxes.

If various local politicians, opinion-formers and journalists thought Delaney might now keep a lower profile and become more amenable, however, they would be sorely disappointed. Had she simply collected her financial windfall and followed Walter Greenwood to transplant herself in some leafy Kentish village down south, then all might have blown over once *A Taste of Honey* faded from the scene.

But Shelagh Delaney was going nowhere. Salford was her town and it would have to deal with her and her opinions for a considerable time yet.

NOTES

1   *SCR*, 12th December 1958.
2   Ibid.
3   *SCR*, 20th June 1958.
4   Ibid.
5   *SCR*, 25th July 1958.
6   *SCR*, 23rd January, 1959: 'A Taste of Honey Has a Bitter Flavour'.
7   *SCR*, 13th February 1959: 'A Taste of Cash for Shelagh But a Kick in the teeth for Salford'.
8   *SCR*, 20th February 1959.
9   Ibid.
10  Ibid.
11  Ibid.
12  Ibid.
13  Ibid.
14  Ibid.
15  Ibid.

16  *Manchester Evening News*, 14th February 1959.
17  *SCR*, 27th February 1959.
18  *SCR*, 10th April 1959.
19  Ibid.
20  *SCR*, 23rd October 1959.
21  *SCR*, 5th February 1960.
22  *SCR*, 15th April 1960.
23  *SCR*, 29th April 1960.
24  *SCR*, 20th February 1959.

# 9

## Ken Russell's *Monitor*

Thanks to generations of Council planning and housing apparatchiks Salford has lost its unique identity as a city, and with it maybe even its soul.

**Nigel Pivaro,** *Salford Star,* **May 2010**

In late September 1960, Delaney took part in a radio conversation in the BBC Home Service in a programme entitled *Ten O'clock.* Along with Arnold Wesker and John Osborne she confronted the critic Cyril Connolly to discuss 'Connolly's Second Law': that literary success often leads to literary failure because it takes the writer out of the environment which first inspired him or her to write. Ironically, the environment that had inspired Delaney in the first place was at that moment being systematically swept away.

By the end of the Second World War, Salford, like other industrial parts of Britain, had a backlog of six years' postponed maintenance of the built environment. Nearly 2,000 homes had been destroyed or damaged beyond repair while an additional 28,000 had experienced lesser damage. As Heather Norris Nicholson, writing in the *Manchester Region History Review* in 2001 observed, "The concept of refurbishment would not enter housing policies for another twenty years and relocation to new over-spill areas was small-scale. Instead, planners sought technical solutions for the needs of the local residents. Housing clearance and renewal schemes were perceived as the means to tackle problems of dilapidation, poor infrastructure."[1]

By the end of 1954, some 1,000 new houses had been built in the city and two years later the first high-rise block of flats, Clement Attlee House, was opened. Another 22,000 slum dwellings were cleared between 1955 and 1975, and by the end of the 1970s it was reported that 44.3% of all homes in Salford had been built since 1944. Between 1955 and 1985 1.5 million slum houses and flats were cleared involving some 3.7 million people: 25 per cent of pre-1914 stock had been demolished.

Per capita, more dwellings were demolished in Salford between 1955 and 1965 than in any other city in the nation, leading one observer to note: "There can be few places in Britain which have been so comprehensively altered in such a short time." There was little official doubt as to the desirability of such massive changes. As a city authority housing publication confidently pronounced in the early 1960s, it was a time when "the little house around the corner was to be replaced by the shops down below."

Nicholson writes, "Through this long-drawn-out process of redevelopment, the locality was transformed and its physical fabric and social character, long noted for a strong sense of community based on close association through family, friends and workplace as well as social and cultural activities was irrevocably altered."[2]

Whole neighbourhoods, set out in grid-iron fashion with smoky Victorian back-to-back terraced houses separated by narrow entries were falling victim to the bulldozer.

What's more, along with substandard housing, many magnificent buildings that served the community were also swept away. Cinemas, churches, banks, department stores, small shops, pubs, social clubs, surgeries, public baths and libraries (including the one on Regent Road where Walter Greenwood had penned *Love on the Dole*) all disappeared.

This revolutionary social experiment in the lives of ordinary people, undertaken on a massive scale, was mounted by engineers, planners, architects and politicians. Those most directly affected were rarely, if ever, consulted. "It was the spirit of the times: a period of prolonged government involvement in planning and public policy making, fired by a vision of enlightenment and modernity to be achieved through urban renewal and *non-consultative decision-making*."[3]

Those responsible for making the decisions were generally up-beat although occasionally defensive. Councillor Albert Jones, Chair of Salford's Planning and Development Committee (who would later be stripped of office for corruption), was reported as saying in early 1960 that the new developments were "in line with what's being done everywhere else",[4] while another councillor judged that it was a "case of modern ways to meet modern needs". When the plan to create a vast shopping precinct in Salford which local traders were fighting along with the local MP was debated, the City Engineer commented: "There is in some quarters an understandable reluctance to abandon old and known conditions for the new and unfamiliar but if such reluctance were always to prevail no progress would be possible."[5]

Where housing was concerned, people were obviously keen to be re-homed. Week after week as new tower blocks went up and familiar districts were cleared, the *Salford Reporter* noted the enthusiasm, if occasionally mixed with some regret and perhaps a little foreboding.

In May 1959 it featured the first families moving into the high-rise Kersal Road estate. 'Browning House Thrills Them', said the headline, beneath which were photos of mothers being given a cup of tea by the flat superintendent's wife. The local pub had been demolished but everyone was reportedly "just happy" to have somewhere decent to live. In August the headline ran, 'Houses Piled on Houses – They're Super!' Twenty-eight families had moved into the newly completed ten-storey Ennerdale House in Ordsall Lane, "and after a week there wasn't a grouse from any of them – but oh those baths and that hot water!"[6]

It seemed the paper, like most official bodies, was firmly on the side of such changes. It even had an in-house local poet, Mary T Malloy, whose verses regularly extolled the destruction of slum dwellings that she and others considered shameful.

> But now I see a Phoenix rise
> With wings outspread across the skies.
> I watch the great sky-scrapers climb
> Where once dwelt poverty and grime.
> You see from Salford's changing face
> The slur of 'slum-town' we'll erase.
> We're building such a city centre
> That we will all be proud to enter.[7]

Even Walter Greenwood himself was quoted regarding the need to obliterate Hanky Park, where he had lived and where *Love on the Dole* had been set, and put something better in its place. "And I believe that in the years to come people will look back and say, 'They did a good job of work in those days.'"[8] However, if Salford had hoped that their newest celebrity writer might also fall into line and cheer on the new developments, they were in for a shock.

New Year 1960 saw Shelagh busy, staying in London with friends and working on the script of the film version of *A Taste of Honey*. She was also working hard to finish a new play called *The Glory, Jest and Riddle*, which would, she said, have the same setting as *A Taste of Honey* and be "rather naughty".[9]

In July of that year, *A Taste of Honey* opened at the Manchester Palace Theatre, but Shelagh wasn't there to see it. It wouldn't be until September, however, that it was announced that her new play, now titled *The Lion in Love*, would premiere in Manchester before travelling to various other cities before its opening in the West End.

As we shall see, *Lion in Love* would see Shelagh launching herself into the theatrical world without Joan Littlewood or Theatre Workshop behind her, the new play being produced by Wolf Mankowitz. Mankowitz had great faith in the play and, along with Oscar Lewenstein, in Delaney as a future star writer. His promotion of her when *A Taste of Honey* came to the West End had seen her image and personality disseminated more widely and effectively than any other new writer in stage history.

Throughout the process, she had remained defiantly herself. For *Lion in Love*, however, Mankowitz persuaded her to go a little bit further. The *Daily Mail*'s Paul Tanfield gossip column announced in September:

> In the past Miss Shelagh Delaney, author of *A Taste of Honey*, has tended to triumph despite her appearance. In the business of mink and Dior dresses she was untidy, lank-haired, a girl with a Left-Bank look. "Smart clothes stifle me," she would say, hitching up her paint-stained jeans. Well, things have changed. Along came Mr Wolf Mankowitz, a man who knows the value of maintaining a good front, to present her latest play, *A Lion in Love*. Something, he decided – preferably a Pygmalion job – would have to be done about Miss Delaney. So, despite her protestations – "I want to look different, I have my clothes made in Salford …" – he sent her along to Charles Creed, one of London's top fashion designers. To see if he could do the trick.[10]

According to Tanfield, Shelagh protested when offered a three-quarter-length coat lined with beaver lamb. "It's unwholesome", she claimed, "to wear dead animals."

They finally settled on a suit in khaki and black boasting a tapered skirt, button-down pockets, and three-quarter sleeves. Its price: 90 guineas. Her picture subsequently appeared in the *Mail*, Shelagh looking rather like a smart West End typist. This prompted the *Salford Reporter* to protest that "any fashionable woman could fit herself out for far less than 90 guineas and complete all her shopping within the city's boundaries."[11] To support the contention, they sent the Salford Carnival Queen, Miss Francis Joy, out as a potential customer to ten "typical

Salford establishments" to kit herself out – for £32! Good fun, perhaps, but one can hardly imagine John Osborne or Harold Pinter undergoing the same 'Pygmalion' process.

Mankowitz's expert hand would next be detected in something rather more substantial to help publicize the launch of *Lion in Love*. It was another piece of prime-time television, but instead of Dan Farson's quirky populist *Success Story*, it would be budding film-maker Ken Russell's BBC *Monitor* programme that would showcase Delaney, her new play and, more specifically, Salford itself.

Russell had been hired in early 1959 by Huw Wheldon, head of the BBC's *Monitor* arts series as a replacement for film-maker John Schlesinger, who was filming *Billy Liar*. In the succeeding three years, Russell made twenty-one short documentaries in the most prolific period of his entire career, before achieving widespread fame with his ground-breaking musical documentary, *Elgar*. *Shelagh Delaney's Salford* was his eleventh feature following *Miners' Picnic*, which had taken him to Northumberland to look at a colliery band contest.

The Delaney film opens with the playwright walking along Salford's main street, then running with her dog Micky down by the canal before entering her home in Duchy Road to sit in her front room at a table prepared for tea. Huw Wheldon's voice-over mentions her two plays set in Salford, "this grey industrial town *near Manchester* ..." and tells us that Shelagh has lived here all her life, that it's the only place she knows thoroughly, at which point Shelagh ceases slicing bread, looks up at someone unseen off-camera and starts her monologue. She agrees with Wheldon, adding that, although she travels abroad now, she is always homesick for England and Salford. The film now starts to intercut her monologue with shots of Salford taken from on high, of misty, smoky old-fashioned back-to-back terracing, gradually descending into the streets, docks and markets.

"The peculiar thing about Salford is that it's like a terrible drug," she continues, "and you might like to get away, *want* to get away and there are lots of people who do, but you can't, for lots of different reasons. For me, it's always a question of coming back."

There follows a sequence in which Russell tracks his camera through Salford's bustling Cross Lane market-place (one of the key features in the new play, *The Lion in Love*) to the strains of a trad jazz soundtrack by the then wildly popular Temperance Seven. As we watch people milling around stalls where the stall-holders are haggling over their wares, Shelagh's voice-over continues,

"For a writer a place like Salford is worth its weight in gold … it's got everything a writer could want … people who live here have a terrific vitality … you've only got to go down to the market to realise that the whole place is alive, there's people teeming into it all the time, buying and selling, haggling and quarrelling. I think it's a fabulous place and the language is alive, it's virile, it lives and it breathes and you know exactly where it's coming from, right out of the earth …"

She then identifies particular characters we are looking at on film: "… That's Mary and her clothes store. We always used to pass the market on our way to the pictures on a Saturday afternoon and we'd buy two ounces of jelly-babies or a toffee-apple or whatever else to take to suck at the pictures and it's funny when you come to think, that the people who are working on the markets now are the same people who were working on the markets then."

The mood then changes as Russell cuts to the docks where Shelagh is seen standing looking out at various ships, her hair waving on the wind as she continues, "… yet at the same time, somehow or other, it seems to be dying …" We are then shown various derelict sites, churches and pubs primed for demolition, as she continues, "… and so much seems to be old, crumbling and neglected. It's a dirty place, too, I suppose but at the same time it's dramatic …"

We see a man standing looking forlornly out onto a busy road as Shelagh continues, "but the thing about Salford is that it can mean many different things to many different people, but to me, at the moment, it means one thing, and that's restlessness. So far as that's concerned, I've tried to write a play about it, but whether I've succeeded or not is beside the point. Everybody, or shall we say young people in Salford, are the most restless people, they're all tethered, they're like horses, to me, like I was, like a horse on a tether, jerking about, waiting for someone to cut the tether … and let me off, let me go."

She then launches into a controversial topic, one that would bring inevitable criticism down upon her head:

"This is the thing about the whole place, people are moving from it, they're tearing down whole parts of Salford and building them again, they're tearing them down but they're not putting the people back, they're sending them away, far away, to places where there's no city, sort of sterile places, and it's a terrible thing to have to start off from scratch …"

Here Russell's film shows us some of the newly constructed Kersal Flats, shot from a moving car as Shelagh continues, "To start from scratch more or less in a new place, so new, nobody knows anybody in it. They're building these places [but] they never seem to think of putting anything in them like a theatre or something, and this is terrible ..."

She then backs this up with personal reminiscence: "We had the same experience when we moved onto this housing estate. Nobody knows anybody and it takes years and years before you can ever get the contact, the same contact, that you have when you lived in a little area somewhere like Trafford Road. There's no neighbourliness, [and] it takes years to do this and I think it's this sort of thing that makes people restless ..."

As if this wasn't bad enough, she then turns to her own disjointed educational experience and attacks the selection system which, according to her, left young people with little opportunity other than office work, or, "They've got three alternatives: they either stay where they are and come to a compromise with the situation; they fight it; or they get away from it. A lot get away, they move and they come down from the provinces and they finish up in London or any other big city [where] they're just as lost and they shouldn't be lost ..." It was, she concludes, a "tragedy".

She then returns to her new play explaining, "... this is more or less what the play is about, because you get three sets of people: old people who've done that, they're restlessness is over; young ones [who] are just about embarking on their careers; but in the middle you get the chaos of middle age when you know it's too late to start again and it's too early to give up, that's all there is to it and it's sad ..."

She concludes by suggesting that she has perhaps been "presumptuous" to talk about people and the city in the way she has but that the city is still "like a rock".

Nevertheless, "I couldn't live here all my life, I'd be too restless, [here she is seen entering Salford railway station] and while I get things out of the city, and it gives me things and I hope I give it something [there is a shot of a steam train belching by] at the same time, no matter what I do or wherever I go, I think I shall always be a very restless person" (and the film ends to the sounds of trains and jazz music).[12]

In many ways, it was a peculiar little film, contradictory, inflammatory and almost serving as Shelagh's farewell note to her home city; if not quite that, then a suicide note where her own popularity was concerned. Unlike *A Taste of Honey* this was unashamedly a Salford portrait. It was not just about 'the North' and not simply a collection of specific characters confined to a cramped bedsit: this was an analysis of the city's present plight and many of its people by one of its most prominent citizens. With its references to Salford being a "dying" place, "old,

crumbling and neglected" not to say, "dirty and smelly", with her criticism of its re-housing policy – not to mention its education system –
coming at a time when controversial policies were being argued and
agonised over, it appeared to be a attack on the whole local council and
its work.

Sure enough, the day after *Monitor*'s transmission, the *Manchester
Evening News* ran a piece beneath the headline, 'Salford Slays Shelagh's
Film': "Salford folk were apparently 'furious' and the 'city's civic pride'
had bristled at the film's drab depiction of itself. The mayor of Salford,
Alderman Miss Margaret Whitehead, was said to be 'disgusted' although
there would be no official protest from the corporation." The report
quoted a "Mrs Ethel Reid, aged 65, who has a shop on Bolton Road,
Irlam's the Height" saying, "Salford is getting stamped with Shelagh's
label and we don't like it." Her neighbour, Mrs Hilda Barrow, a member
of Salford's arts committee, said, "Why doesn't Shelagh Delaney give us
a programme showing the better places in the Height, Broughton, and
Buile Hill Park?"[13]

The *Salford Reporter* itself soon weighed in, complaining, 'Does TV
always have to splash the black side?' claiming that many angry citizens
had phoned the town hall and a 'flood' of letters had arrived almost all
condemning her vision of the city.

"What a poor presentation of Salford and what an impression to give
those seeing the programme in the South ..." wrote one, while another
wondered why the film had concentrated on "shots of grimy chimneys,
docks, and a dirty river".[14]

The city's Director of Education felt that, though sincere, Shelagh
was talking for a tiny minority and at times contradicted herself. Even
Mary Crozier, the *Guardian* television reviewer, felt that her 'theory'
concerning 'restlessness' was confused, that she wasn't particularly
articulate and that it might have been better if she had simply "described
what she saw".[15]

A friend of Shelagh's, one Arthur Taylor, wrote a long letter in her
defence making the point that "... amid these sordid surroundings,
reminding one of a brick jungle, are the warmest, friendliest people that
live anywhere in the country. They can make a total stranger feel like a
member of the family in the twinkling of an eye. To me these people
could show the rest of the country how to live as one, and I am sure this
is how Shelagh sees Salford and she shows these feelings in her plays."[16]

Taylor was almost alone, however, apart, inevitably, from Shelagh's
loyal mother. "All was quiet today in S's home in Duchy Road, Pendleton

and her mother could not understand what all the fuss was about. 'I thought it was a lovely film,' she said."

Meanwhile, the play that was to encapsulate many of the strands of thought articulated by Delaney was about to appear. Salford held its breath …

NOTES

1 Heather Norris Nicholson, 'Two Tales of a City: Salford in Regional Filmmaking, 1957–1973'. *Manchester Region History Review*, 15 (2001), pp. 41–53.

2 Ibid.

3 Ibid.

4 *SCR*, 26th February 1960.

5 *SCR*, 19th February 1960.

6 *SCR*, 21st August 1959.

7 *SCR*, 24th April 1964.

8 *SCR*, 26th February 1960.

9 *SCR*, 12th February 1960.

10 *Daily Mail*, 19th September 1960.

11 *SCR*, 4th November 1960.

12 BBC *Monitor* film, 15th September 1960.

13 *Manchester Evening News*, 26th September 1960.

14 *SCR*, 30th September 1960.

15 Quoted in *SCR*, 30th September 1960.

16 *SCR*, 30th September 1960.

# 10

## *The Lion in Love*

None of the women playwrights who followed Shelagh possessed a fraction of her four-square-plain gifts and poetic realism. Yet at the age of twenty, she was savaged with such deliberation and spite that her successors would have run howling to some lunatic Equal Opportunities Tribunal.

John Osborne, An Autobiography, 1991

To some at the time it was a mystery why *The Lion in Love* would not be produced by the Theatre Workshop company at Stratford. Ossia Trilling, the American critic who was on the board of Theatre Workshop for over ten years, suggested some time later that the play had been rejected by Littlewood "after fruitless attempts at doctoring the text".[1]

This does not quite accord with Littlewood's own version of events: "… a package arrived from Shelagh Delaney. It was her second play, *The Lion in Love*. I read it with growing disappointment. It had more characters, less appeal and even less shape than Honey. She had learned nothing from the company's adaptation of her first work."[2] Littlewood says she wrote back to Shelagh, "Read a good play, an Ibsen for example, then analyse it, note the construction. Play-writing is a craft, not just inspiration."

Shelagh replied, "If you aren't interested enough in my play to sort out the good from the bad, and generally put me right where I've gone wrong, then I may as well be working on it with the people who think that there is enough stuff there to be doing something with. I know you were only considering my play because more important things, like Brendan's new play, weren't ready yet."[3]

With that, Delaney's creative involvement with Theatre Workshop ended. Instead, she turned to Wolf Mankovitz who, with partner Oscar Lewenstein, had taken *A Taste of Honey* into the West End. The move would lead Delaney, ultimately, into the camp of Littlewood's declared enemy: the Royal Court.

*The Lion in Love* is a three-act play set squarely, unambiguously in Salford. The title of the play is taken from an Aesopian fable in which a lion permits a forester to remove his claws and teeth as preconditions for marrying the forester's daughter. Once he submits, the forester kills him. The moral: "Nothing can be more fatal to peace than the ill-assorted marriages into which rash love may lead."

Compared to *A Taste of Honey*, *The Lion in Love* is both more compressed in terms of time-span (it takes place over just three days spread across several weeks) and more diverse in terms of characters. Her range has been extended to include an entire family, the Freskos: grandfather Jesse, his daughter Kit and her husband Frank, and their children, Banner and Peg; then there is Nora, who is having an affair with Frank; Loll, Peg's boyfriend and fiancé; plus Andy, an injured acrobat and pimp, and Nell, a prostitute.

At its heart, given the title's origin, is marriage, both existing and proposed. Kit and Frank's is faltering, ostensibly because Kit is a good-time woman who is for ever going off to get plastered in pubs and then being arrested as drunk and disorderly. Why she does this is not explained. Frank is clearly involved with another woman, Nora, but it seems as a reaction to Kit's waywardness. Nora's offer to Frank, that he should leave Kit and set up with her elsewhere in a small shop, is one of the play's few dramatic hooks: will he leave or not? In the end, somewhat predictably and with little real explanation, he doesn't. Peg, meanwhile, is being courted by Loll, a Scottish fashion student, and at the end of the play appears to have eloped with him to London. In the meantime, Kit and Frank's son, Banner, who appears at the start of the play as a surprise to all, having been elsewhere accumulating enough money to escape to Australia, does eventually leave – without saying goodbye to his mother who is lying indoors in a drunken coma. Nell and Andy have plans to create a new acrobatic performance act but these are blighted at the end, Andy being revealed as not as good a dancer as Nell had thought.

Grandfather Jesse, meanwhile, spends the majority of his time on stage commenting on his progeny or reminiscing about better times. Although various characters confront opportunities for fulfilment, most of them lose their chance through either hesitation or fear. The action consequently seems either directionless or circular, with little external change.

There is the suggestion that *Lion in Love* possesses autobiographical elements in that it deals with the temptations and opportunities of the wider world and the traps that await you should you not take the chances offered and get out. Freedom is a constant ideal: one that education can offer if it is provided properly; one that marriage can crush if you stay too long with the wrong person; one that 'art' can provide but only if its good enough.

For the play's director, Mankowitz turned to someone with little experience at such a level, 28-year-old Theatre Workshop graduate Clive Barker. Barker was then at the start of a long and distinguished career in the theatre, both as a director and teacher. He had appeared in Brendan Behan's *The Hostage* in 1958 and would later feature in Littlewood's greatest triumph *Oh! What a Lovely War*. Until that point, however, his only administrative job had been stage managing Associated Rediffusion TV's *Cool for Cats*, one of the first shows on British television to feature music for a teenage audience.

Auditions for *Lion in Love* began in July 1960, the roll-call of would-be future stars hoping for a break including Terence Stamp, Sean Connery and Oliver Reed. Kenneth Cope would succeed in securing the main role of Frank. Others selected were Theatre Workshop stalwarts such as Howard Goorney and Diana Coupland plus a good friend of Delaney's, Patricia Burke. Early suggestions that the structure of the play (as predicted by Littlewood) was causing problems come from a letter from Mankowitz to Barker and Delaney in which he says that Act II "fails to resolve the situation towards which I would call the 'pseudo-resolution' on the part of the characters i.e. audience should feel the characters at the end have their own ideas about solution to their own problems."[4]

There were other passages of irresolution in Act II and Mankowitz felt the need to give Kit a very big scene because she has been kept in the audience's eye. There was jealousy between Nora and Kit, and Mankowitz wanted a full-blooded resolution to this. He also suggested that "Frank will [ought to] go with Nora."[5]

Ultimately, there would be attempts by Barker to replicate the rollicking atmosphere of a Joan Littlewood production. A single musical theme and counter-melody played on two guitars entitled 'Delaney's Theme' were used to cover all entrances and exits by characters as well as in several scenes to underline the action. The theme was played in many different styles and rhythms, sometimes as a tango, sometimes as a waltz, a march or a cha-cha-cha, depending upon the needs of the play and the production. It was written by Mankowitz's regular musical collaborator Monty Norman, who later found enduring fame as the composer of the

James Bond theme.

On 29th July it was announced that *Lion in Love* would be produced first at the Belgrave Civic Theatre, Coventry for two weeks followed by two weeks 'on tour' (one of those weeks to be at the Opera House, Manchester where Delaney had been an usherette for six months after leaving school) before opening in the West End.

"What's it about?", the *Salford Reporter* asked. "No one will say." As to why Joan Littlewood wasn't involved: it had been "darkly hinted that Miss L thought it 'too bourgeois'".[6]

In early August, the *Daily Mail* reporter Cecil Wilson caught up with Shelagh at a YWCA club in Bloomsbury where *Lion in Love* was in rehearsal. It was a somewhat downbeat interview, the 'Sagan of Salford' as she was again dubbed, appearing keen to backtrack on her earlier 'fireball' image.

"I talked a lot of rot when I first came to London," she admitted. "I hope I've matured a bit since then." Wilson reported that she hadn't made nearly as much money as the reports at the time suggested and hadn't bought the 'scarlet sports car' that reports at the time had made so much of. She'd compromised with a blue Ford Consul.

When asked what *Lion in Love* was about, she declared, "Oh dear, I'm hopeless at describing my plays. I make them sound so frightful. The new play is set in the north – not Salford necessarily – and it's based on the Aesop fable of the lion who fell in love with the huntsman's daughter. It's a sort of triangle play about a man, his wife, and his mistress and the interplay of their emotions. Does that makes sense? Anyway, I think it's a bigger play than *Taste of Honey*. The people in it aren't quite such shockers. Very bourgeois, I believe the word is."[7]

Bigger it might have been but it very quickly ran into trouble with those who saw its début at Coventry. The *Times* critic commented that though she could write lively and realistic dialogue, there was little or no sign that she was learning to resolve this talk into satisfactory action, while Jeremy Brooks in the *New Statesman*, beneath a headline: 'Chunks of Life' considered the play completely formless and plotless: "The dramatic experience, the thing we go to the theatre for, is not life in the raw – we can experience that for ourselves – but life given a tangible form by art, so that action and meaning have miraculously become one."[8]

John Coe reviewing the Bristol performance thought "Miss Delaney's talent will become increasingly valuable to the British theatre when she succeeds in making the drama less static and her characters something more than mere mouthpieces for her lively line in chatter."[9] John

Mapplebeck, a future BBC producer and director, wrote of the Manchester production: "Stage characters come and go without cause. The play is a series of sketches more than an entity … too often she can be so gauche as to make the gallery, as well as the stalls, squirm with embarrassment for her …" Unfortunately, he concluded, "it still represents the most interesting theatre we have seen in Manchester in the past 12 months."[10]

In a *Guardian* interview on 20th September beneath the headline 'Playwright on Probation', Shelagh appeared unconcerned:

> Surrounded by a clutch of journalists and looking, in a grubby white mackintosh and a hastily tied scarf, her usual determinedly unfashion- able self, Shelagh Delaney was busily parrying questions about her love life and her taste in clothes. A press conference to herald the Manchester opening of her latest play, *The Lion in Love*, had produced a large attendance, for to journalists Shelagh Delaney is the nearest thing to a home-grown, contemporary Garbo. She has not, apart from the tall austerity of her height, anything like the looks, but she has the same talent for creating, almost in spite of herself, racy headlines …

She wasted no time in rejecting the 'slum girl' label that had been attached to her: "My mother has a nice council flat overlooking Salford park and I divide my time between there and London." About the gossip columnists she is only "sad, and has long since given up accepting any responsibility for what they print".

What she was keen to do was establish herself as what she termed "A probationary or an apprentice playwright", one that owed an enormous amount to Littlewood and the Theatre Workshop. At the same time, she rejected concerns about the British theatre being a middle-class theatre and did not accept Arnold Wesker's assertion that theatre-going was only a middle-class habit. "The working classes in the gallery have supported the British theatre ever since Elizabethan times. Give them good and well-publicised plays and they will go to the theatre."

She wanted to attract young people to the theatre and drew some consolation for the bad notices her play had received at Coventry from the fact that it had attracted a young audience. She had what the *Guardian* reporter called, "a bland self-confidence" which put the hostile reception for *Lion in Love* down to the fact that critics expected the play to be "almost exactly the same as *A Taste of Honey*". "I expected bad notices and those I have read, if they had been written about any other play, would make me want to dash out to go and see it."

She was prepared to admit that she might have something to learn about the construction of a play but added that critics who had complained about her technique had missed the point: that her new play is meant to be "loose and sprawling". "I would rather write a terrible play than a mediocre one," she concluded.[11]

A week or so later, however, Mankowitz wrote to Barker and Delaney to say how sorry he was that the play wouldn't get a London opening because he couldn't make a deal for a London theatre.[12]

Two weeks after that,[13] Shelagh was once again explaining to journalists that the apparent failure of her second play was of no consequence. Was it hard for her to swallow? she was asked. No, she was undismayed. She was concentrating on her third play. "It's a shame for the actors of course, but for me it doesn't really matter if it comes to London or not. As far as I am concerned it is a success. I know it is a much better play than *Taste of Honey*. This is the kind of thing you expect for a second effort of any kind. The reviews were not all terrible, and the audiences have been quite good. But we can't get a suitable theatre in London. The West End would have been nice but I'm not really worried."[14]

She went on, "*Honey* is making enough money for me to live on. People have called *Lion in Love* uncommercial. I don't know what that means. If getting them into the theatre and making them laugh and think isn't commercial, I don't know what is … I am not interested in what the critics or even what the mass audience think about it …"[15]

Mankowitz disagreed: "*Lion in Love* is not as good a play as we hoped," he commented, though he added it *would* be commercial in the right theatre; "but the only theatres we could get were too big. We lost money on tour. In the wrong theatre we'd lose even more. I have options on her next two plays and I'm convinced one will be a smash hit."[16]

But things suddenly changed. John Osborne had been (and would be again) dismayed at the way critics had attacked the play. The "obtusely vicious reception" for *Lion in Love* was, he thought, "the classic example of a second play being demolished on the grounds of feigned admiration for a first play's privately resented success".[17]

Lewenstein, Osborne and George Devine had seen the play on its initial run in Bristol, and Devine thought that it should be given a Royal Court run, "as an act of faith in Delaney's artistic talent".[18]

Thus, early in November the English Stage Company re-engaged Barker to put on *Lion in Love*. Rehearsals were set for 28th November, and the play was to open at the Royal Court on 21st December.

Littlewood must have been mildly amused at such a turn of events – the play she had rejected as being a great disappointment was to be staged at her greatest rivals' home.

This time there was a bewilderingly wide range of assessments of it, with critics veering from the wildly ecstatic to the sneeringly dismissive. Tom Milne of the *New Left Review* considered Delaney "the nearest we have ever got in this country to Chekhov",[19] and Albert Hunt thought *Lion in Love* pointed, "towards a new kind of theatre, a theatre of 'pure behaviour'".[20] Bernard Levin lauded her "shrewd and penetrating observations" but thought it a shockingly bad production. "As far as I am concerned, Miss Delaney can have any prize in the stall …" Felix Barker considered it, "a moving play which increases my respect for Miss Delaney as a writer".[21]

On the other hand, Anthony Cookman in the *Tatler* thought *Lion in Love* remained "intractably a banal little play",[22] and Philip Hope-Wallace in the *Guardian* wrote: "… the play itself is a sadly ill-organised affair. The big outlines are missing. The interest aroused is dissipated and from the middle of the second act to the end of the third, the piece trickles away into little or nothing."[23] Milton Shulman meanwhile suggested that her second play demonstrated, "inept professionalism", that most of the time, "it is a plodding bore," and that "With this play Miss Delaney established the fact that she is the most overrated playwright of the decade."[24]

One of her greatest champions, Kenneth Tynan, went into much greater detail, suggesting that it was, "much improved with several loose ends neatly knotted and many rough edges smoothed off the playing".

Authenticity, honesty, restraint and a prevailing sense of humour: these qualities, seldom found in union, are all Miss Delaney's, and I am glad to salute them. Yet something is missing, some proof of focus and selection that was present in *A Taste of Honey*. The new piece sprawls and repeats itself, thus wasting time that might better be spent on explaining *how and why* the lion allowed himself to be disarmed and caged. Grandpa, a walking fund of pawky maxims, should be released from the cast at once, in order to devote his talents to inventing mottoes for Christmas crackers. Quite often – and this is a really damaging charge – one cannot distinguish between lines that are intended to sound banal, and lines that are banal only by accident.[25]

The play would last for just twenty-eight performances before closing. The *Evening Standard*'s 'Londoner's Diary' reported Mankowitz's lament that he "ha[d] lost a lot of money on the venture", but at least its Court run in 1960/1 produced box-office takings of more than twice the production costs.

From a distance of some fifty years one can see that Delaney was trying for a more worldy-wise approach with a group of characters almost all of whom went beyond far beyond her writerly ken.

In *A Taste of Honey* she had needed help from Joan Littlewood and Avis Bunnage with older characters like Peter and Helen. Littlewood had commented: "And it wasn't surprising that a girl of nineteen couldn't make sense of a woman of forty. The mother's boyfriend, Peter, with his white house, park-sized garden, tennis court, swimming pool and bottomless wallet, didn't make much sense either ..."[26]

When she stuck closer to herself, Delaney produced a witty, smart, unhappy, divided character who was compelling to watch. That Jo didn't actually go anywhere or do anything was not the point. We were interested in her. Sadly, it is hard to get interested in any of the characters in *Lion in Love*.

That marriage could prove a constricting bind appeared to be her concern in the play but the complicated business of middle-aged marital angst seems too much for her. It was as though she was watching the characters from outside, with no real idea what was going on inside. (She would return to this theme much more successfully some fifteen years later with a six-part tv series dealing with more or less the same characters as Kit and Frank). In *Lion in Love*, she provides no real reasons why Kit and Frank's marriage has faltered. Kit drinks a lot and is clearly on the edge mentally, but nothing helps us to understand this. Indeed, her husband Frank appears a pleasant chap, so much so that he has guilt feelings about leaving his drunken wife for someone much better off and much more grounded. His reasons for staying are also left unexplored. If they had voiced their concerns in language approaching that which she achieved in *A Taste of Honey* it might have been enough, but she fails to produce very many good lines, as if the effort to create a clutch of significant characters was too much.

Delaney's basic ideas at this point are few. She once said that her writing advocated no political philosophy other than "common sense and kindness", and that the theatre was a place where "the audience has contact with real people, people who are alive." The latter phrase puts one in mind of her contemporary Arnold Wesker, whose Beattie character in the 1958 play *Roots* makes a great deal of wanting to 'live' rather than just exist. Beattie may appear today as hopelessly idealistic and unrealistic, but she voiced her concerns and desires in such a way as to make it clear what was tearing her apart. Delaney's characters in *Lion in Love* appear simply to want 'something else' (Delaney had already made references in the *Monitor* film to people feeling "tethered like horses") but there is no tension created as we wait to see if, for instance, Frank will leave Kit for Nora. The same choice had been at the heart of *Billy Liar*, a contemporary play and film, in which Billy is presented with the opportunity to leave his Northern town and try for fame and fortune down south. His ultimate failure to grasp the opportunity is heart-wrenching but we also know that his fantasy world provides him with a refuge. We gain no such insights into any of the characters in *Lion in Love*.

Writing about dysfunctional families, which the Freskos could be said to illustrate, was also not particularly unusual. *Lion in Love* might be contrasted with another contemporary play dealing with families 'on the margins' written by John Arden in 1958. *Live like Pigs*, about wildly contrasting families settling into new council housing in a northern English industrial town and the mayhem that ensues, was a great deal nastier and more challenging than *Lion in Love*. This is not to suggest that Delaney should have been writing a different play but simply to point out that she was not the only playwright dealing with such marginal characters, and that hers suddenly seemed bland and colourless.

What's more, the addition of Nell, a 'good-time girl' (or prostitute), looks somewhat juvenile. There is no real examination of her situation, simply the statement that she can make good money that way, while her pimp is similarly without depth. Prostitution may well have been part and parcel of Salford life – and still is – but it is so casually included as to seem gratuitous, as if to shock, the suspicion being that Delaney was cocking a snook at grown-ups by doing something provocative (as in those remarks to the *Salford Reporter* about her next play being 'sexy' and 'daring') when it's actually not daring at all.

For Delaney, the play's failure might have been a chastening experience, but if so, she didn't show it. She would stick by *Lion in Love* and a year or so later would take it to New York. For now, something else had irked her, and she let rip in an article in the *Daily Mail* soon after the Royal Court opening.

Beneath the headline, 'Hypocrisy! The National Sport of the English – by its Angriest Critic', she blamed the theatre censors for "spoiling the end of *Lion in Love*".

In fact, there had been a number of small but telling alterations. "Think the sun shines out of your back-side" had become "think you're a little tin god"; "God suffering Jesus" had been altered to, "Good God". But what had irked her most of all was the Lord Chamberlain's refusal to allow the word 'bugger' to appear in the script. Thus: "You dozy buggers" had become, "You dozy devils", but more importantly, the very last line of the play had originally read, "It's a bugger of a life, by Jesus." This had been changed to: "It's a bastard of a life."

She complained: "The Lord Chancellor [*sic*] spoiled the end by censoring a word I used in the last line. A six-letter word. In the North it is almost a term of endearment. It is exactly expressive. But out it had to go. And I had to substitute a much harsher word. Bastard. Used as a description, not an epithet."

"Miss Delaney savagely ground out her umpteenth cigarette and immediately lit another. 'Then there's the terrific sickening hypocrisy about smut. You'll get theatre audiences roaring their heads off at sly innuendoes. But face them with honest-to-goodness sex, and they act as if they were aghast, disgusted ... Hypocrisy', went on Miss Delaney, 'is a mistaken sense of what is valuable. It is pretence for effect.'"[27]

So concerned had she been, that she'd written an insertion into the programme for the London opening revealing that she had had to alter the ending and that it had "weakened the impact in those places where [the omitted words] occur especially in the last sentence of the play where this weakness has already received comment from the press when the play was on tour."

The reviewer in *Plays and Players* indirectly agreed with her: "'It's a bastard of a life' betrays a facile, almost adolescent cynicism that makes one feel that Miss Delaney needs to develop more as a person than a playwright before setting to work on her third play."[28]

Peter Lewis in the *Daily Mail*, however, dismissed her "rather pompous programme note", concerning the censor's change to the end: "But it wouldn't have helped, Miss Delaney, it really wouldn't have helped."[29]

NOTES

1  Ossia Trilling, 'The New English Realism', *Tulane Drama Review*, 7, 2 (Winter 1962), pp. 184–93.
2  *Joan's Book.*
3  *Joan's Book.*
4  Clive Barker Archive.
5  Ibid.
6  *SCR*, 29th July 1960.

7   *Daily Mail*, 12th August 1960.

8   *New Statesman*, 17th September 1960.

9   John Coe in the *Bristol Evening Post*, 16th October 1960.

10  John Mapplebeck in the *Guardian*, 29th September 1960.

11  'Playwright on Probation', *Guardian*, 20th September 1960.

12  Clive Barker Archive, 29th September.

13  *Daily Mail*, 15th October 1960.

14  *SCR*, 21st October 1960.

15  Ibid.

16  Ibid.

17  John Osborne, *Almost a Gentleman: An Autobiography*, vol 2: *1955-1966* (Faber, 1991).

18  Speech by Anthony Dunn to the Art Workers Guild on 13th November 2008, commemorating Wolf Mankowitz.

19  *New Left Review* (November/December 1960).

20  *New Left Review* (January/February 1961).

21  Bernard Levin, *Daily Express* and Felix Barker, *Evening News*, 31st December 1960.

22  *Tatler*, 18th January 1961.

23  *Guardian*, 31st December 1960.

24  *Evening Standard*, 31st December 1960.

25  *Observer*, 1st January 1961.

26  *Joan's Book*.

27  *Daily Mail*, 1st January 1961.

28  *Plays and Players* (January1961).

29  30th December 1960.

# 11

# Delaney's Theatre

Clive Barker and Shelagh Delaney want to do for Salford
what Joan Littlewood tried to do for Stratford East. Miss
Delaney has apparently received the parting advice from
Joan Littlewood that she should go back to Salford and
write as many plays as possible.

*Salford City Reporter*, August 1961

The failure of *Lion in Love* didn't halt Shelagh's onward progress.
Whether or not an Angry Young Woman, she was certainly a Busy Young
Woman, working on her new 'historical' play as well as the film script
for *A Taste of Honey* – which had been postponed from the previous year
and would be filmed in the city to be released later in 1961. In America,
the Broadway production of *Honey* opened requiring new material while
a radio adaptation of the play would be performed on the Third
Programme (Radio 3) by the Manchester Library Theatre repertory
company. Shelagh would also be in demand for TV and radio
appearances, and would write an introduction to a book of L.S. Lowry
paintings while also finding time to travel in late October 1961 to Poland,
then still a communist country.

She wrote about the trip in a chapter called 'Vodka and Small Pieces
of Gold' included in her prose collection *Sweetly Sings the Donkey*
(published in 1963).

Poland at the time was experiencing something of a small revolution
in cultural matters. Following the suppression of the Hungarian uprising
of 1956 had come the Polish Thaw (or Gomulka's Thaw) after the Soviet
Union had granted the Polish leader some concessions following
workers' protests at events in Hungary. The Polish Writers' Union thus
became more of a bona fide writers' organisation devoting itself to
creative output and the well-being of its members rather than

promulgating government-imposed 'socialist realism'.

Her trip was ostensibly tied in with a production of *A Taste of Honey*. She was a guest of the Polish Writers' Union, stayed at their guest house in Warsaw and was officially expected to visit theatrical centres and meet Polish actors and directors. Instead, she appears to have treated the visit more like a tourist jaunt than a cultural exchange. Seemingly unfettered by officialdom, she travelled alone by plane and bus to the extreme south of the country to Cracow and thence to Poronin in the Tatra Mountains, the 'Polish Alps', and the country's principal tourist region. (A press photo has her posing with local 'mountaineer poet' Andrzej Skupień-Florek.)

Shelagh had not come for the skiing or hiking, rock climbing or cave exploration, however. Poronin was where a significant Lenin museum was then situated, the great Russian revolutionary having frequently visited the place in the early part of the century. By her own account, however, she had spent all her money by the time she got there and couldn't afford the admission fee.

Nevertheless, while not being a card-carrying communist, her views during this period were consistently leftward-leaning. She had already started to appear at radical gatherings in London. In December 1960 she was part of a distinguished group of artists, including Henry Moore, Vittorio De Sica and Federico Fellini, who were said to be setting up an international club to "fight the medieval survival of illiberal laws" and state censorship. On 10th April 1961 she was heard speaking her mind on a BBC radio programme concerned with the class system in Britain: "Conversations with Miss Shelagh Delaney, Mr Alan Sillitoe, Mr Dennis Potter and Mr Malcolm Bradbury were, one supposes, a fair view of traditional British radicalism," reported *The Times*.

There was also her increasing involvement in various peace movements which were pressing for an end to nuclear weapons during a particularly tense Cold War period. In February 1961 a letter she had written to the Salford Peace Committee was published in the *Salford City Reporter*. It was vintage Delaney: "It is becoming more and more obvious that the pressure we and other people in the world who are not prepared to be led to the slaughter like a flock of sheep are exerting on the uncertified lunatics who want to see us all heaped up on the nearest bone-yard is being felt."

It wasn't right, she felt, that while half the world was dying of hunger, "planes carrying death should shadow the sky ... death-carrying submarines should skulk in the sea ... But I believe that the politicians and the newspapers are waking up to the fact that the Campaign for Nuclear Disarmament (CND) is not being organised by a group of fanatical cranks and eccentrics but by truthful and sincere men and women whose only fanatical belief is that there must be and can be peace on earth."[1]

She followed this up by becoming one of the leading lights of a World Without War exhibition mounted at Height Public Hall, King Street, Salford. Actors Patricia Burke, Christine Hargreaves (of *Coronation Street*), Margaret Leighton, Dame Sybil Thorndike, Albert Finney, Tony Warren and others including Joan Littlewood, were all recruited as sponsors, while speakers included Mr R.W. Casasola, President of the Foundry Workers Union and Professor Bernal, a distinguished scientist and president of the World Peace Council (WPC).

The fact that the WPC was an organisation sponsored by the Communist Party of the Soviet Union to promote peace campaigns around the world in order to oppose 'warmongering' by the USA, and that Bernal was an unreconstructed Stalinist who had failed to condemn the Russian suppression of the1956 Hungarian uprising, not to mention the resumption of Soviet nuclear tests in the same year, seemed not to bother Shelagh.

Later in the year she would take part in the first mass CND demonstrations in central London, would be prominently photographed doing so, and finally arrested along with John Osborne and Vanessa Redgrave. The novelist and playwright Doris Lessing recalled: "Before that Sunday [of the demonstration] I had two visits. One was from Shelagh Delaney who said she hated demos and riots and even large numbers of people massed together, but she supposed she had to do it? My sentiments exactly."[2]

The demonstration happened to come a day after the premiere of the film version of *A Taste of Honey*, where John Osborne, a firm advocate of passive resistance, was quoted as saying, "I want to be jailed." He would get his wish. Along with a number of prominent artists and writers including George Melly, Allan Sillitoe, Ronan O'Casey and Patricia Burke, Osborne would spend the night in a cell after a sit-down protest. Delaney and Vanessa Redgrave were also held overnight before appearing at Bow Street magistrates' court the next morning. As they left the court, Redgrave linked arms with Delaney, the two of them having been fined £2 each, and declared: "We will take part in any future demonstration. We will go to prison if necessary …"[3] Shelagh Delaney, however, was quoted as saying, "I don't want to go into a police station any more."[4]

Nevertheless, Shelagh remained a keen supporter of all things radical, a stance that would not endear her to the establishment in her home city. This would become painfully apparent during her attempt to establish a 'community theatre' in Salford, a venture arising out of the Centre 42 movement led by playwright Arnold Wesker.

Centre 42 had its origins around Christmas 1961 when a group of creative people from the theatrical world came together in London to discuss their dissatisfaction with the prevailing commercial ethos of the theatrical world, as well as what they felt was the isolation of actors, painters, musicians and other artists from the wider working-class public they wished to reach. The group included Wesker, Bernard Kops, Sean Connery, Mordecai Richler, Delaney, Sean Kenny, Clive Exton and Doris Lessing. They discussed the possible acquisition of a warehouse in Covent Garden and the establishment of a free space in order to explore new modes of expression, to put on overlooked foreign plays and to initiate workshops. It was to be community-centred, if not based in a community centre as such, and was intended to serve as a reaction to the "hopelessly conservative" commercial theatre.

The name Centre 42 derived from Resolution No. 42 at the 1960 Trades Union Congress calling for an inquiry into the state of the arts. The hope was that the trade union movement would become engaged in helping to stimulate working people into promoting and taking part in the provision of the arts themselves.

In 1961 the Trades Council of Wellingborough in Northamptonshire invited Wesker's organisation to help them mount an arts festival to encourage union recruitment. This was followed by five other Trades Councils (Nottingham, Birmingham, Leicester, Bristol, and Hayes & Southall) inviting Centre 42 to mount arts festivals in their cities. This positive initiative galvanised Salford trade unionists into approaching Shelagh for help with a similar local initiative. She turned to Clive Barker, who happened to be involved in the day-to-day running of Centre 42.

In March 1961 the Salford community scheme was launched, the *Salford Reporter* running a headline, 'Shelagh Would Back Community Theatre'. The idea thus became closely associated with her from the very start. In fact, Barker was keen to place her at the forefront: as he told the *Reporter*,

Shelagh wants to leave London and have a company and theatre of her own. It may take three or four years to do it. That requires a big act of faith on Shelagh's part. She would be prepared to back it to an extent but we want the community to own the theatre. It would be a place for plays, concerts – jazz and classical – and a focal point for the community where all sorts of cultural activities could take place.

But we are not ramming culture down people's throats. We have got to find out what Salford wants first and that's where Shelagh comes in. She will canvass her friends and all sorts of people in Salford and see what they want before we rush into anything. It needn't necessarily be Salford but it would be an ideal spot in which to start because of Shelagh's connections with the place and knowledge of it. Certainly no other place would be considered unless and until Salford was finally discarded.[5]

At home in Duchy Road Shelagh added: "We want to have a theatre that is looking forward all the time instead of backwards and one that would be more closely identified with the people living round about than even local repertory companies are."[6]

For some months during the summer of 1961 there was much enthusiasm for the idea. Meetings were held at Delaney's Duchy Road house involving local councillors, religious leaders, youth workers and some local businessmen. Financial plans were drawn up and published, along with details of who would be employed, how much tickets would cost, break-even figures etc. Even the type of plays to be produced was outlined, a possible early cause for some misgivings amongst local politicians.

The new theatre would provide, "a wider range of plays than Manchester Library Theatre", which, like similar repertory companies, presented work outside the interests of local industrial populations and which pandered to, "remnants of the old middle-class …"

The *Salford Reporter* pointed out that 'Shelagh Delaney and Barker believed that the territory explored in *A Taste of Honey* and *Lion in Love* could be investigated further and that a whole new theatrical tradition could be created in Salford. They wanted to see plays about the lives of the people of Salford, that their ideas included a playwright who would be apprenticed to the company but they insisted that the theatre would not concentrate exclusively on 'this type of social realism'."[7]

For those sceptics delving deeper into the idea, however, the name of Roger Planchon, mentioned on a number of occasions in statements and written agendas by Barker, would have given them pause for thought. A French working-class writer, Planchon had formulated his own complex Marxist style and approach to theatre performance (critics likened the freshness and vitality to Joan Littlewood's productions) and in 1957 he took over a large municipal theatre in Lyon located in the working-class suburb of Villeurbanne where he proceeded to build a 'people's theatre' that aimed to bring culture to working-class audiences beyond the Parisian boulevards. This was considered as a possible model for Salford.

The key to it all, however, was a suitable building. According to Delaney's plans, it was essential that it would not be just an old-fashioned performance space. Audience members would be encouraged to stay on after particular shows and discuss them. It would be a place where people might meet; a centre of community life, open all hours.

Top of the list was the Salford Hippodrome, otherwise known as the Windsor Theatre, although from the very outset Barker appeared to concede that the chances of getting it were remote, particularly as the present owner, when approached by the *Salford Reporter*, admitted that he'd only ever heard of Shelagh Delaney by name, that he'd not been approached by the community theatre committee and that if present negotiations with unidentified parties went through, "it is unlikely the Hippodrome would continue to be used as a theatre."

Barker pressed on, nevertheless, convinced that the old building could be restored. From March through the summer and into the autumn, the discussions and planning proceeded. It came as something of a shock, therefore, when, with no prior warning, the council bought the Windsor for £10,000 – not with a view to restoring it but in order to knock it down.

In the council chamber, some councillors were surprised that it had cost so much to buy a derelict building that might have been compulsorily acquired anyway. In fact, the theatre didn't feature in any of the current development schemes. However, during the council meeting to discuss the purchase, the latent animosity towards the "Delaney plan" was clear.

"It is not proposed to buy it for a Civic Theatre," Alderman F. Cowin stated. "While some of them wanted a Civic Theatre, they [the council] did not want the sort of thing that had been talked about, with professional producers, actors, prompters, doorkeepers, and with the Corporation paying for them. They [the council] would in time get a theatre which could be used by the people of Salford." He then urged councillors to "stop reading mysteries into a perfectly simple issue. We have not even discussed the question of its use as a civic theatre."

The leader of the council and future mayor, Alderman Hamburger (owner of the Salford firm Searchlight Electrics, an electrical wholesale business), went further in moving the resolution to buy it, urging the council to erase from their minds everything they had heard and read about the activities of a "group of high-minded people. They [the council] need it for redevelopment and they want it now in order to stop it being used for something else."

He added that there had never been any chance of central government giving consent for a theatre idea anyway, hinting that money would never have been forthcoming for the Delaney plan.[8]

Nevertheless, it looked like an extremely expensive pre-emptive strike. One of the original proposers of the scheme, Arthur Taylor, was in no doubt as to the motivation: 'Politics Killed Delaney Theatre Plan', ran the headline beneath his letter to the *Salford Reporter* some months later: "It has been said about the Theatre Group that it was inspired by Communism. This is one of the most childish statements ever to come from people who are supposed to be intelligent citizens."[9] Though overstating things somewhat, Taylor was close to the mark. The Centre 42 Movement itself would founder, largely because the wider labour movement, being traditionally conservative where cultural issues were concerned, was suspicious of its radical nature, not to mention its middle-class overtones. Salford's council would be similarly sceptical of the Delaney plan.

What could not be denied, however, was the anti-Delaney sentiments prevalent on the council chamber. Councillor Jack Goldberg, who had been in favour of the scheme, but was also involved in trying to set up a simpler theatre project, wrote to Barker in the New Year:

> I think I also ought to state at this stage that I have been surprised in the last few months to find out how much prejudice there is amongst members of the council against Sheila on the grounds that her plays have brought Salford into disrepute. As a result this means that any project with which she is known to be connected starts off at an enormous disadvantage when we ask for Council support and it may be advisable in any future Civic Theatre project we have to back pedal her interest in the matter. I am extremely sorry about this not least because my views on her work differ from those of many of my colleagues but I think it is best to be forewarned about this.

Even the estate agent involved in searching for a suitable property for the project agreed that "there seems to be a strong feeling against Shelagh Delaney from many people."[10]

Barker refused to accept Goldberg's suggestion. "I am not prepared to compromise in the face of what I consider bigotry and pretend that Shelagh Delaney is not at the heart of the venture." He pressed on for a month or two, looking at other sites, but without council blessing, the idea was effectively dead.

In the months that followed, certain prominent Salfordians made their feelings abundantly clear about Delaney. Alderman Hamburger said in a speech that the "persistent denigration of Salford by all sorts of people for all sorts of motives" made him "want to vomit ... I don't understand why there seems to be a general policy of denigration of this city when anything worthwhile is in issue by all sorts of people – whether playwrights drawing royalties from plays on subjects which seek to rub our noses in the muck or aspiring playwrights who have learned from others' successes."[11]

In June, the magistrate Noel Capindale, a significant individual in local union affairs who had taken part in discussions about the project at Delaney's Duchy Road home commented, "I'm hoping that some day Salford will produce a playwright who will put the city in its true perspective and not as in *Love on the Dole* and *A Taste of Honey*."[12]

Canon Hussey, meanwhile, the much-respected rector of Sacred Trinity church, in a Sunday sermon made reference to the "false image of Salford" conveyed by local writers and artists.: "... a gross distortion with no resemblance to present-day truth".[13]

Shelagh made no further comments on the failed project but would later return to her battles with local councillors in an oblique, but quietly stated fashion.

NOTES

1   *SCR*, 3rd February 1961.
2   Doris Lessing, *Walking in the Shade* (Harper Perennial, 1998), p. 366.
3   *Daily Herald*, 19th September 1961.
4   *Daily Telegraph*, 19th September.
5   *SCR*, 3rd March 1961.
6   Ibid.
7   *SCR*, 18th August 1961.
8   *SCR*, 6th October 1961.
9   *SCR*, 26th January 1962.
10  Letter to Clive Barker, June 1962 (Clive Barker Archive).
11  *SCR*, 17th April 1962.
12  *SCR*, 1st June 1962.
13  Ibid.

# 12

# Filming *Honey*

Just photographing an existing stage production – however successful – is bad cinema ...

Tony Richardson, in *The Cinema of Tony Richardson, 1999*

Throughout the long months of Salford's community centre saga, a film version of *A Taste of Honey* was being prepared and shot in and around Salford itself. Ironically, given the endless complaints concerning the play's deleterious impact on the city, with its emphasis on the old and decaying rather than the bright and the new, Tony Richardson's achievement would be to present the city to the world as a strikingly beautiful object. The film would be an international success at the box office and further imprint an image of Salford – and the North – on the minds of millions. It wasn't the first film during these years to venture into that mysterious, exotic world beyond Watford.

*Room at the Top* in 1959 was the pioneer in a new wave of British films all set in northern England and with largely working-class protagonists. *Saturday Night and Sunday Morning* followed in 1960 starring Salford-born Albert Finney; then came *The Loneliness of the Long Distance Runner* and *A Kind of Loving* in 1962, *This Sporting Life* and finally *Billy Liar* in 1963.

Loosely dubbed "kitchen sink" movies, they were all serious films with artistic pretensions. Shot in black and white and directed by men of the calibre of Lindsay Anderson, Tony Richardson, Karel Reisz, John Schlesinger and Jack Clayton, they utilised some of Europe's finest cameramen and technicians. However, although considered classics of their kind, none apart from *A Taste of Honey* would be associated so closely with a particular place.

Richardson was no typical film director. After a successful run of directing plays at the Royal Court Theatre, he had become interested in making films, principally of a documentary style. Along with fellow Royal Court directors Lindsay Anderson and Karel Reisz, the cinematographer Walter Lassally, director Lorenza Mazzetti and the technician John Fletcher, he had formed a group dedicated to producing what they termed Free Cinema. This was cinema without propagandised intent or deliberate box-office appeal. The movement began with a programme of three short films at the National Film Theatre, London on 5th February 1956. Five more programmes appeared under the Free Cinema banner before the series was ended in March 1959.

Anderson explained in a manifesto for the movement: "These films are free in the sense that their statements are entirely personal. Though their moods and subjects differ, the concern of each of them is with some aspect of life as it is lived in this country today. Implicit in our attitudes is a belief in freedom, in the importance of people and in the significance of the everyday."[1]

As with their work in the theatre at the Royal Court, their aim was to reform the prevailing conditions in which artists worked. They aimed to break down what they termed the 'bourgeois' (that is, conforming to prevailing middle-class standards) restrictions of theme and style that were suffocating creativity. Then it had been West End theatre; now it was mainstream British cinema and its all-pervasive parochialism that they were determined to circumvent. They wanted to make director's films, not industry films.

"We were not interested in treating social problems so much as we were in becoming the first generation of British directors who as a group were allowed to work freely on material of their own choosing ..."[2]

In 1958, along with John Osborne, Richardson took his objectives a step further with the formation of Woodfall Films which aimed to combine the key principles espoused by Free Cinema and the Royal Court. Osborne nominated Richardson to lead the assault "on the suburban vapidity of British film-making", their first project being to bring Osborne's *Look Back in Anger* to the screen.

Having snapped up the film rights to *A Taste of Honey* as soon as it had opened in Stratford East in 1958, they quickly found money to finance new ventures scarce. The American company Warner Brothers, for instance, had only put up the money for *Look Back in Anger* when the international film star Richard Burton agreed to play the lead role of Jimmy Porter. It subsequently failed at the box office. They then turned to the British Bryanston consortium of independent British producers to finance *The Entertainer*. Despite having Laurence Olivier in it, that also

*Top left:* Tony Richardson directing Rita Tushingham and Paul Danquah.
*Top right:* The 'Ugly Duckling' Rita Tushingham spreading her wings during a break in filming.
*Bottom:* Murray Melvin, Rita Tushingham and the real Salford.

**A Taste of Honey hits the Silver Screen in 1961.**

failed to make money.

Although determined to make films with as little interference from Hollywood as possible, Richardson found himself flirting with Hollywood for a while with predictable results. The American producer Harry Saltzman considered *A Taste of Honey* "too provincial and too English", while another American producer – Darryl Zanuck – though happy to finance *Honey* added ridiculous provisos. According to Richardson, Zanuck read it and offered to do it but on one condition, that there was a happy ending. Richardson replied that there already was such a happy ending, with Jo awaiting the birth of her baby. Zanuck responded: "That's the point – the baby's gotta die, and the mother and girl go off to a better life." Richardson continued his search for money alone.[3]

A year later, however, with the help of Bryanston, a British film company formed by Michael Balcon and Maxwell Setton in mid-1959 following the collapse of Ealing Studios, he produced Karel Reisz's first feature, *Saturday Night and Sunday Morning*. It was with the profits from this film that he and Woodfall were able to set up the production of *A Taste of Honey* in the way he wanted – with no American studio strings and as an all-location film.

On 11th March 1961 he told *The Times* that *A Taste of Honey* would be "an experiment in neo-realism more complete and far-reaching than has yet been attempted in a major British feature film: there will be no studio work at all, and the whole film, interiors as well as exteriors, will be shot in surroundings corresponding exactly to those depicted in the play, shot completely on location."[4]

As we have seen, *A Taste of Honey* when produced as a play by Theatre Workshop, had been confined almost entirely to one small room. When Littlewood had first looked at the original script, she had commented sardonically: "I skimmed the pages. A section of a street, the main entrance to a house, a living-room with two doors and a window overlooking the river, a bedroom, a kitchen. It needed a film unit."[5]

The film version of *Look Back in Anger*, directed by Tony Richardson who would also be the director of *A Taste of Honey*, had been largely confined within the four walls of Jimmy Porter's claustrophobic attic flat, apart from a couple of scenes in the local market and a graveyard. A film version of *Honey* might well have been expected to be just that: a camera following the characters from one part of the room to the next, maybe next door. However, Richardson had been unhappy with the resultant clash of styles in *Look Back in Anger*: the pseudo-documentary location shooting for the exteriors, had not mixed well with the mannered theatrical nature of the indoor scenes. He was determined not to go down that route again.

As we shall see, this would have far-reaching consequences for Delaney's original idea. When Richardson said he was going to make an all-location film, he really meant it. The majority of the film takes place outdoors with many significant dramatic moments occurring against a Northern (predominantly Salford) backdrop of canals, tenement buildings, pubs, docks, ships and fairgrounds, starry skies and rain-swept piers. The only internal sequences, those set in Jo and Helen's bedsits, were filmed in London. *The Times* reported in April 1961 that Richardson was using a derelict house off the Fulham Road for them. However, cameraman Lassally revealed some years later that they used the scenery workshop of the Royal Court Theatre for the loft-like second flat that Jo rents when pregnant. This was an ironic twist of fate, given Joan Littlewood's scorn for the Court and all its works. Joining forces with Richardson and Woodfall had marked a definite shift away from the ethos and guidance of Littlewood's Theatre Workshop for Delaney. It would also involve a decisive break with how her play and its possible meanings had been realised by Littlewood.

Before starting filming, however, the choice of actors, especially the casting of Jo, would occupy some considerable space in the popular press. The original American backers had wanted Audrey Hepburn, but Richardson was determined to cast an unknown actor, just as he had done so successfully with Albert Finney for *Saturday Night and Sunday Morning*. The search became notorious for John Osborne's suggestion that they were looking for "an ugly girl" to play Jo. Quite why he had settled on such an idea is hard to fathom, particularly as the character of Jo was based, in spirit, on Shelagh herself. Not surprisingly, the search proved difficult. According to Richardson,

> All the actresses who had played it in the theatre were far too old for the film. We started an immense search. It was very thorough: first photographs, then interviews, then readings or improvisation and finally a full-scale film test. I saw well over 2,000 girls. I'd short-listed the best and still felt unconvinced. Out of nowhere a young girl called Rita Tushingham turned up from Liverpool. She wasn't very prepossessing. The only experience she'd had was being the hind legs of a donkey in a local pantomime.[6]

Tushingham had been working at Liverpool Rep when she saw an article in the *Daily Express* announcing that John Osborne was seeking "an ugly girl for *Taste of Honey*". According to Tushingham, her brother Colin said, "Go on, Reet, have a go, you're ugly enough!"[7] In the initial auditions she did not impress, but at the last moment Richardson saw something in what he called Tushingham's "*all-speaking* eyes" and she was selected. It was a crucial decision. According to William L. Horne, "Much of the overall impact of the film [*A Taste of Honey*] stems from the mesmerizing shots of Rita Tushingham's eyes."[8]

Although some press reviewers would be unkind to her, likening her to "Donald Duck's sister" (after the film-makers had foolishly announced that they'd found their 'Ugly Duckling') and commenting on her 'waddling' backside, the film would propel Tushingham to stardom in an oddly similar way to Delaney's own meteoric rise. Both were teenagers (Tushingham was just seventeen when making the film) and their similarly 'unusual' looks played a considerable part in the popular press's reaction to them.

Where the rest of the cast was concerned, there were fewer problems. None would be established stars. Murray Melvin would be the only member of the original stage play to be selected for the film, reprising his role as Geof. Helen would be played by Southport-born Dora Bryan, an experienced stage and screen actress who specialised in stereotypical female character parts and with none of the high profile of some of the actresses who'd played Helen on stage, such as Angela Lansbury and Avis Bunnage. Peter would be played by Bristolian Robert Stephens who had been appearing at the Library Theatre in Manchester when George Devine spotted him and brought him to the Royal Court when setting up the English Stage Company. There he'd subsequently appeared in John Osborne's *The Entertainer* and *Epitaph for George Dillon* and Arnold Wesker's *The Kitchen*. The 'Boy' would be played by Paul Danquah, a part-time actor and law student who came to Richardson's attention via the painter Francis Bacon.

Where the actual script was concerned, it would cause fewer problems with the censors (this time the British Board of Film Censors) than the play had done. Just like those employed by the Lord Chamberlain's office, the readers were unimpressed by the storyline, one commenting, "I think it is more credible now but I still don't feel it comes from the heart; more like a semi-poetic fancy concocted by someone young and inexperienced (which indeed Shelagh Delaney is). Anyway, from our point of view it seems a fairly straightforward 'X'."[9]

The X was merited, apparently, because of the "extreme youth of the central character" and her pregnancy ("we would not want to have a possible complication of what I might perhaps describe as a *Lolita* element"), some of the language used and Geof's homosexuality.

Where the latter was concerned, John Trevelyan, Secretary of the Board, commented: "We have never had any ban on homosexuality on the screen but, bearing in mind that the cinema-going public is in the main very different from the theatre audiences, we usually suggest that where it is not a main theme but is incidental, it should be suggested rather than directly shown."[10]

He pointed to a section in the script where it was suggested that a child might imitate Geof's way of walking. "It might be rather unpleasant if it is markedly mincing in a homosexual way," Trevelyan thought. Murray Melvin, who played Geof, thought the same. Melvin has always been proud of his performance in that he played Geof as a real person rather than a caricature. He claimed in later years that he had disagreed with Richardson on set when the latter had repeatedly called "Cut!" in a scene where Geof steps out of a shoe shop. "You're not swinging your hips," Melvin says Richardson told him. He claims he refused and insisted on playing it his way.[11]

William L. Horne, on the other hand, felt that Richardson's bisexuality, which was not publicly known until many years later, "helped him to direct this character [Geof] with delicacy and tact" and that his direction, "benefits from an intuitive sympathy for the social outsider".[12]

For the City of Salford, the arrival of the film cameras caused a ripple of excitement. The *Salford Reporter* of 17th March ran a headline, 'It's a Busy Life for Shelagh', noting that Shelagh herself had departed for America to see her play on Broadway and to make a number of personal appearances. At the same time, the film unit production team had based themselves at the Midland Hotel, the technicians at the Grand Hotel, while the cast were using Milverton Lodge as their headquarters. The report advised readers, "Don't be surprised if you feature in the final film. [The production supervisor] is so determined to use 'real' people in everyday settings that he is adopting – in part – the 'Candid Camera' technique while on location in Salford and Stockport."[13]

The decision to shoot the film completely on location was not simply because the funds were available: it was also *technically* possible because of the availability of newer film stock. The director of photography for the film would be Walter Lassally, a key figure in the British New Wave who'd come to Britain as a refugee from Nazi Germany. After shooting a number of documentaries and shorts, several for Free Cinema directors, including Karel Reisz and Tony Richardson's *Momma Don't Allow* (1955), Lindsay Anderson's *Every Day Except Christmas* (1957) and Reisz's *We Are the Lambeth Boys* (1959), he followed these directors into feature films and contributed to the look of the new British realist cinema of the late 1950s/early 1960s. *A Taste of Honey* would be his first major feature film. He would go on to make many more significant movies, including *The Loneliness of the Long Distance Runner* (1962) and *Tom Jones* (1963), and would win an Oscar for his work on *Zorba the Greek* (1964).

For *Honey*, he decided to use three different film stocks: HPS, Ilford's newly available highest-speed film dubbed "the fastest film in the world", for interiors such as Helen and Jo's first flat. The much less sensitive, more fine-grained FP3 film for exteriors, plus a third film stock, HP3 to link the scenes. By relating the film stock to particular sets, or décors, Lassally made the granularity of the film stock become part of the art direction, something nobody had ever done before. He was advised by the film laboratories that it wouldn't work, but he insisted. "And it was okay in the end," he concluded.

Lassally was particularly proud of his work on *A Taste of Honey* and later complained when it was bundled together with other films of the period that had working-class, everyday subjects and were dubbed the 'kitchen sink school'. This, he felt, underplayed *Honey*'s 'poetry'. While it treated working-class problems, it treated them, he insisted, "in a highly poetic manner. It's not at all a strictly realistic view. It's very much a romantic view and the film is a very atmospheric film. And it's also a very poetic film."[14]

He was concerned, of course, with the look of the film, something he had worked extremely hard to achieve. His point of view, that *A Taste of Honey* was more than just a "grimy slice of life" would be confirmed by the majority of critics who saw the film in late 1961. Paul Dehn in the *Daily Herald* felt that it fulfilled Richardson's, "poetic promise and avoids the technical pitfalls of *Look Back in Anger* and *The Entertainer*".[15]

The *Guardian* reviewer felt that "the words have, so to speak, been taken out of the small stage set and put into the large, drab yet picturesque hurly burly of a northern industrial town (the town is Salford)."[16]

William L. Horne was moved to defend this 'picturesque' aspect of the film however as, "not ... merely decorative" claiming that it "provides an authentic and believable environment for the characters".[17]

Alan Dent in the *Sunday Telegraph* agreed, and considered that "this brilliantly directed film … really does take us to Salford, steeps us in such a town's way of life, and makes us take a far deeper interest in the characters than we could do in the play."[18]

The *Times* reviewer wrote: 'The shabby streets and wet pavements, the school playgrounds, the public monuments and the rubbish-strewn canals – even the worn headstones in the churchyard, 'sacred to the memory of' – are seen as an integral part of the story. The background is always alive and always changing; but the visual image is in keeping with the spoken word. We accept implicitly that these characters have grown naturally and inevitably from out of these surroundings."[19]

This aspect of the film would come in for some criticism, as we shall see. But where the film world in general was concerned, *A Taste of Honey* was a big success. It won the 1961 British Film Academy Awards for Best British Film, for Best British Screenplay, for Best British Actress (Dora Bryan), and for Most Promising Newcomer (Rita Tushingham).

And to confirm Lassally's point of view, it also won a prestigious 'art-house' award at Cannes, sharing the Special Jury Prize with *The Trial of Joan of Arc*, directed by Robert Bresson, and *Eclipse*, directed by Michelangelo Antonioni. When the rest of the cast and crew had to leave the ceremony before the certificates were handed out, Lassally stayed behind to collect them. "When I finally got hold of the certificates they were supposed to be signed by the festival director and they weren't signed. And I thought, 'Oh my' – so I signed them myself. With a squiggle."[20]

NOTES

1   From David M. Robinson, *The History of World Cinema* (Stein and Day, 1973), quoted in Jo M. Welsh and Jo C. Tibbetts (eds.), *The Cinema of Tony Richardson: Essays and Interviews* (SUNY Press, 1999).

2   Colin Gardner, *Karel Reisz*, British Film Makers, new edn (Manchester University Press, 2012).

3   Welsh and Tibbetts, *Tony Richardson*.

4   *The Times*, 11th March 1961.

5   *Joan's Book*; Welsh and Tibbetts, *Tony Richardson*.

6   Welsh and Tibbetts, *Tony Richardson*; William L. Horne, 'Greatest Pleasures: *A Taste of Honey* (1961) and *The Loneliness of the Long Distance Runner* (1962)'.

7   *Daily Express*, 27th April 1960.

8   Welsh and Tibbetts, *Tony Richardson*.

9   Aldgate, *Censorship and the Permissive Society*.

10  Ibid.

11  http://britishlibrary.typepad.co.uk/archival_sounds/2012/06/murray-melvin-on-the-theatre-workshop.html (recorded 12th July 2006).

12  Welsh and Tibbetts, *Tony Richardson*.

13  *SCR*, 17th March 1961.

14  http://www.webofstories.com/Walter Lassally.

15  *Daily Herald*, 15th September 1961.

16  *Guardian*, 16th September 1961.

17  Welsh and Tibbetts, *Tony Richardson*.

18  *Sunday Telegraph*, 17th September 1961.

19  *The Times*, 13th September 1961.

20  http://www.webofstories.com/

# 13

# Salford Sublime

The film's real heroes are Mr. Richardson and his masterly cameraman Walter Lassally, who between them have caught Manchester's canal-threaded hinterland to a misty, moisty, smoky nicety.

Paul Dehn, *Daily Herald*, September 1961

The stars of the film would ultimately prove to be Rita Tushingham and, thanks to Lassally's camerawork, Salford itself. However, despite the fact that Delaney collaborated closely on the script (Richardson and Delaney would share the scriptwriting award) it would be Richardson's personal vision that came to dominate the film. In adapting the play, Richardson had not simply opened it up and taken it outside. There was, on his part, a clear intention to reveal what he felt was the 'truth' in Delaney's story, something he felt Littlewood's theatre production had obscured. It was clear from comments made by those involved at Woodfall that they had never been 100 per cent behind Joan Littlewood's interpretation. John Osborne, even when defending it, had commented: "An *overemphatic production* still did not succeed in completely distorting its basic truthfulness and quality."

Richardson himself felt that the technique of mixing working-class drama with 'pub vitality' and vaudeville songs as Littlewood had done could be effective in staging plays such as Brendan Behan's *The Hostage*, but that her technique had worked less well on *A Taste of Honey*, where it made the play seem coarse and "forcedly jolly". These devices, he thought, had clashed violently with the naturalistic tone of much of the dialogue. Of other innovations such as characters speaking to the audience: "The effect seems both mannered and self-consciously avant-garde. It is joined by another annoying idiosyncrasy, the use of music and dance to effect scene changes ..."[1]

Thus, in writing the screenplay, Richardson and Delaney "abandoned

Littlewood's 'self-reflexive tics' in favour of a *complete naturalism*. Far from merely opening up a stage play, they aimed to transform the piece into a work for the cinema."[2]

The film opens with shots of Jo reluctantly playing netball in her school playground. It's made clear that she is moving home again – behind on the rent, mother and daughter are then seen running away from their landlady and crossing over town by bus to new, bleak lodgings in a slum area. On the way we see them looking out somewhat ruefully at municipal buildings, statues and a variety of street scenes.

When they arrive at their new lodgings, a young black man (Jimmy) helps Jo off the bus with her cases. Two sequences then establish Peter, Helen's new boyfriend – at work in a used car dealership, and later in a pub where Helen entertains the clientele singing to piano. We next see Jo in school, listening to literature being intoned by a teacher, but she mocks her, entertaining the class just as her mother had entertained the pub clientele. (There are echoes here of Shelagh's own classroom antics.)

Later, after detention for her clowning around in class, we see Jo fall down some steps leaving the school and hurting her knee. There follow extended scenes of Jo walking along the canals, watching barges, and finally reaching the dock quayside – to the accompaniment of 'The Good Ship Sails on the Alley Alley O'. She then meets Jimmy again coming down the gangway of the ship where he is a cook. Their subsequent courtship takes place largely outdoors, often with canals as backdrop.

He treats her injury on board his ship and they play hide and seek along its decks. The film cuts to a dance hall where Helen and Peter are jiving to a dance band. Back then to Jo and Jimmy, who eventually kiss beneath the stars. The film fades and we are looking up at a different type of stars – those on the ceiling of a dance hall where Peter and Helen are still dancing, slowly, cheek to cheek. Peter asks her to live with him. Helen makes a key remark: "You certainly liberate something in me and it's not maternal instincts either."

We then watch Jimmy and Jo part. Next day he meets her outside school and walks her home. They declare their love for one another and both are seen dancing away, like children, playing hopscotch. When Jo comes home, Helen tells her she will be getting married and that she and Peter will be going to Blackpool. Jo insists that she comes, too. Cut back to the canal, where Jo is given a ring by Jimmy. We then watch Jo and Helen and Peter and friends set off for Blackpool.

The group visit all the tourist attractions but Jo is cheeky and troublesome throughout, enraging Peter. Helen eventually agrees to send her home. Back home, she meets Jimmy waiting outside the lodgings. They spend the night together, and in the morning she walks to the docks with him and watches him board his ship and sail away.

Helen returns from Blackpool and the longest of the original scenes from the play takes place in the bedsit with the revelations about Jo's father. Crowds of children that now appear chanting and singing as Helen leaves will play an increasing part in the film. We then see Jo working in a shoe shop and renting a large, derelict flat in the slum district. Geof enters the shop and she serves him, selling him some shoes. They later meet by chance watching a traditional Salford Whit Walk parade. After a trip to the fair, she brings Geof back to her new flat. Later they go for a day out in the country where Geof tries to kiss Jo.

Later, after her pregnancy is established, Geof goes to an antenatal clinic and is given a doll for Jo to practise with. There are further location scenes by the canal, in a graveyard and then inside Helen's new house when Geof comes to tell her that Jo needs help with her pregnancy. Apart from one more visit to the canals, this time by Geof and Jo, the rest of the film takes place as in the play, inside Jo's bedsit.

At the end of the film, we watch Geof as he stands in the yard outside the flat watching the local children put a guy on a lighted bonfire. One of the children gives Jo a sparkler to hold. The final scene in the play is between Jo and Helen alone, whereas the concluding sequence in the film concerns all three and is shot partly from Geof's point of view; indeed, the penultimate shot is of Geof. He sees Jo appear on the other side of the fire, but she doesn't see him and he leaves, unseen by Jo and the children.

Cameraman Walter Lassally found the location filming both challenging and exhilarating. The extended Blackpool scenes, for instance, were filmed without a great deal of pre-planning, documentary-style and all in one day. He explained: "In Blackpool we had a severe weather change. It started fine and then it clouded over and became rainy. We could see this about to happen so we decided to shoot the first part of the sequence second, all the hand-held stuff of them walking along the Promenade in Blackpool amidst the holidaymakers with just a few extras whom we insinuated behind the main players ..."

Often the film crew simply stumbled across interesting sideshows and attractions and decided to seize them: in particular "an extraordinary performance with a woman being garrotted and a sort of strange stage show where a half-nude girl is on the bed ... and the hall of mirrors which isn't easy for camera but it was managed ..."

He was also very lucky on occasions. Filming a sequence with Jo and

Geof beneath a railway viaduct with Jo silhouetted against the sky in the fading light proved difficult. "Below the knees I needed something light so I had a lot of light-coloured sand put down ... And then the weather came to our rescue. In fact, at the beginning of this sequence, which starts under a railway viaduct in the city, the weather change matched the mood change exactly and happened right on cue, so that as Jo and Geoffrey manage to pull out of their gloom and cheer up, and she says, 'We're extraordinary people, you and I' and they run through the arch deciding to go for an outing in the country, the clouds part and the sun breaks through. Now this can obviously not be planned, it's just luck and I've found generally that luck is an essential ingredient in the best planned of schedules."[3]

His hard work paid off, however. Richardson's intention to make something entirely different from Littlewood's theatre production convinced the film critics, many of whom felt that his version of *Honey* was far superior to the play.

Isabel Quigley in the *Spectator* wrote: "It is hard to imagine, if you never saw it on the stage, *how it was ever anything but a film*. Alleys, docks, churchyards, shopping streets, backyards, the canal, the sky, the weather, ships and buses and prams are all so intrinsic a part of its speech and action that it hardly seems they could have existed on their own between four stage walls."[4]

In fact, Delaney's original story was considered lacking in vital respects by many critics: "The weaknesses are all from the play (dialogue etc.) not in the adaptation or its photography."[5] "Against this industrial setting Mr. Richardson has told Miss Delaney's story. Its faults are still apparent. The plot is still shapeless and inconclusive – indeed it is little more than an anecdote of city life, with a beginning but no end – and the characters often seem to lack consistency. But there is heart in the telling, and an intense realism in the situation."[6]

Paul Dehn in the *Daily Herald* felt that Richardson's "film version of Shelagh Delaney's black little Lancashire comedy knocks spots off the stage production by Joan Littlewood who among other mannerisms kept making the actors speak lines to the audience which they ought to have spoken to each other."[7]

Not everyone at the time felt that the transfer from stage to screen was a success. John Russell Taylor felt that too much time was wasted in what he termed, "useless illustration and explanation": "The special quality the play has of just letting things happen, one after another (like in a dream) disappears and modifications [Richardson's 'uncompromisingly realistic and exterior' treatment] clearly intended to strengthen the material succeed, paradoxically enough, only in making it seem thinner and more contrived."[8]

Some two decades after the film's release, Russell's point of view was given some heavyweight support. Film historians Andrew Higson and John Hill were unconvinced that the 'picturesque' elements of the film that so captivated 1960s critics added anything at all to the original story. Rather like Russell, they felt the myriad shots of town and country slowed things down and, instead, "obliged the viewer to pay attention instead to the film's pictorial beauty ... For narrative drive we substitute the pleasure of spectacle – townscapes made picturesque, squalor aestheticised."[9]

Hill asserted: "It is place, rather than action, which assumes importance."[10] Higson felt that the brilliant camerawork, especially "That Long Shot of Our Town from That Hill" (a view, like that of the opening credit shot of *Coronation Street*, from 'outside and above'), opened up a broad chasm between the observing eye of the camera and that of the observer within the landscape. It was, moreover, a class-based viewpoint, middle class in particular, maybe even a Southern-based middle-class, which saw the North as an alien place, "and the people as potentially threatening, dangerously strange. But the images are also beautiful, picturesque: the poetic in British film culture is both beautiful and strange. The self-conscious aestheticisation of the landscape erases the danger, the traces of the otherness, rendering it an exotic and spectacular landscape ..."[11]

The captivating beauty of the scenes as rendered by Lassally thus turned (middle-class) audiences into voyeurs. As a consequence, Higson felt that they would be too carried away by the splendid visuals to feel any sympathy for the characters or to care about their problems. Furthermore, in spite of its ambition to document and poetically portray the working man and woman, the 'kitchen sink' film genre, of which *A Taste of Honey* was a prime example, ends up increasing the distance between viewers and viewed: "The distance is disavowed; the impenetrability of the real living city is transformed into a surface, a representation, an image which does not need to be penetrated, but which can be gazed at precisely as image: the fascinated, fetishistic gaze."[12]

Twenty years on, such a line of thought may seem overly didactic. More pertinently, although we (who view the film?) may find the various backdrops of the city captivating, we are always engaged in the emotions and dilemmas of the characters occupying those scenes, in particular Jo. Rita Tushingham's expressive face (what one reviewer termed her "wonderful, eloquent eyes") and her uncanny ability to capture every moody nuance of a fatherless girl stuck with a fly-by-night mother whose main goal in life is to have a good time, hold us throughout.

If Richardson's (or rather Lassally's) cameras roam across Salford from on high, they also relentlessly close in on Jo's face, on Helen's, indeed, on all the characters' faces, for Richardson has a remarkable way of getting his actors to reveal themselves through all but wordless close-ups. If we *are* voyeurs, then it is in the sense of being 'flies on the wall', intruding upon mother–daughter scenes of great intimacy and pain.

Delaney said sometime later in another context, "Aren't all women Madonnas if they are married and have children?"[13] Helen, as played by Dora Bryan, is a real mother who, despite her apparent fecklessness, wields great power over Jo. We can see this more clearly in the film than in the play, as Richardson is able to capture the sudden changes of mood more starkly with his close-in camera work then would be possible in a theatre. At one point Jo blurts out at Helen that she is a liar. Helen turns in the act of making her face up and stares coldly at Jo and says simply, "Am I?" Jo's defiant look crumbles into fearful compliance. "No," she says meekly and Helen turns away, her mother's power having been proved. Jo's desperate need for her mother is demonstrated throughout and she generally loses: on the pier at Blackpool, though she venomously insists on her right to be possessive, she is sent home like a naughty child.

At the same time, the film version alters the original ending, shifting the emphasis from the renewal of Jo's relationship with Helen to the severing of her relationship with Geof. This renders the central relationship of the play version, that between mother and daughter, more ambivalent in the film. It had already been altered, of course, when Jo moved out and found herself her own place to live. In the play, Helen retained control of the situation because although she leaves, she still controlled the rent-book. Once Jo left, however, she was more her own boss.

If there is a theme running through the film/play that Richardson has been able to develop, however, it is the contrast between the world of the adult and that of the child. This is emphasised by his increasing use, as the film progresses, of crowds of small children. This irritated some reviewers: Albert Hunt writing for the *Universities and New Left Review* was particularly scornful:

> Whenever Richardson takes the camera out-of-doors streets, graveyards, fields and hills seemed to be filmed with picturesquely-dirty children playing singing games. Nowhere is Richardson's tendency towards abstraction more irritatingly apparent. The children are not included because they are interesting and alive. They are atmospheric props, part of the pseudo-poetic blur.[14]

The presence of the children has been variously interpreted as: signifying a romanticised, unsullied past; serving as a constant reminder to Jo of what she is about to be burdened (or blessed) with; commenting on the action through the words of their playground songs.

Yet the young adults in the film also play like children: Jo and Jimmy playing hide and seek on the boat, hopscotching along pavements, fiddling with toy cars; Jo and Geof reciting nursery rhymes to one another, running off to the countryside in the company of the said children and later struggling in vain to cope with the impending birth of Jo's child. The vast majority of the outdoor scenes involve the young adults while, apart from their Blackpool excursion, Helen and Peter remain indoors. This only emphasises the sense of power the adults (in particular mothers) assume in the film; adults live indoors; children play outside.

There were, however, other more important aspects of Richardson's approach to the text that subtly altered its original theme and intention. Nadine Holdsworth felt that Joan Littlewood's production had skilfully avoided a danger inherent in the play, that of "nostalgic sentimentalism". Littlewood, being an unrepentant Marxist, had refused to denigrate working-class life and culture, "as plays such as *Look Back in Anger* and Arnold Wesker's *Roots* (1959) did, as inferior and lacking credibility".

Holdsworth explained: "Rather than presenting an extended lament for a lost culture of extended families and close-knit communities, it [the play] maps a different experience of individuals who live wholly in the present moment as they collide to create alternative, often temporary, family units. Through its heightened music-hall-style theatricality, vital language and sharp wit it lifted what could have been a drab and tragic story of poverty, neglect and wasted talent into another realm."[15]

By contrast, there are moments in Richardson's film when his New Left concerns for the way in which a shoddy new consumerism was just then starting to transform working people's lives becomes apparent. Helen and Peter represent a form of working-class aspiration both derided and feared by the middle-class left: their new kitsch bungalow, his drunken 'loadsamoney' bragging, the gross images of the couple and their friends on their trip to Blackpool: all could be seen as a critique of mass leisure, something absent in the play.

> We are given close-up shots of Helen and Peter and their friends as they cavort around the funfair, with an angle of vision and closeness to the face that produce similar visual distortions to those of the hall of mirrors. A grotesquely dressed-up Jo, unwanted, bloody-minded, and trailing a few yards behind, offers a point from which the spectator can position him/herself in alienation from the scene while, just in case we haven't got the point, the whole montage sequence is accompanied by raucous pop music and the loud, empty laughter of a mechanical clown.[16]

Richardson's concentration on the 'naturalism' of the play, on its 'realism', albeit 'poetic' also has the effect of leaving the viewer somewhat sadder and less hopeful than did the exuberant Joan Littlewood interpretation. Littlewood had always expressed a deep dislike for 'realism' and the set for *A Taste of Honey* had been deliberately designed in a non-naturalistic style; thus her version of *Honey* had "vibrated with a different kind of life, an eminently theatrical but still wholly unrealistic life", according to one critic.

Music, song and dance had removed it even further from 'real life'; yet it communicated something life-affirming in its exuberance and vitality. Kenneth Tynan had gone as far as saying: "It deals joyfully with what in other hands might have been a tragic situation."

For the underlying tale is not a happy one; instead, it documents "the cycle of the single mother trapped in poverty with the inherent possibility of neglect starting all over again for the child about to be born". For Edward Esche, considering the play script three decades after its first performance, the play illustrated "abuse breeding abuse ... the jokes simply serve the function of papering over or disguising a pattern of social fracture, and thereby deepening rather than negating the tragic experience." Tragic, "because no solution was offered to the cycle of decay".[17]

What Richardson could not replicate (indeed, was clearly trying to avoid in his rejection of what he called the "forcedly jolly" nature of Littlewood's production) was the sheer fun of the Theatre Workshop production; the humour and the slapstick were avoided, and a character like Peter, for instance, whom John Bay in the Littlewood production created as a droll, comic character, extremely funny and very welcome in the rather lachrymose story, according to Littlewood became increasingly nasty and abusive as the film version proceeded. Helen, as played by Dora Bryan, becomes a wonderfully scatty, good-time girl but her treatment of Jo is much less distanced than the Helen of the play. Bryan's Helen always looks as if her sympathies are with Jo, that her waywardness is just a silly affectation, ready to be dropped the moment her daughter needs her. This makes for a more sentimental film; in fact, the lasting impression of Richardson's film must be a melancholic one, wistful rather than defiant.

As Nina Hibbin, of the *Daily Worker* put it, "… the total impact [of the film] is of emptiness and human defeat. There are no real peaks of delight. Its fatalistic ending leaves everybody as they were – not sadder, not wiser, not better, not worse: no more capable of coping with life than before."[18]

Inevitably, the way in which *A Taste of Honey* is understood today is largely via Richardson's film. Though the play is regularly revived, it's the 1961 screen version that people most often refer to, being the most accessible. Ironically, Hill and Higson's criticism of the film – that Richardson had made Salford look aesthetically picturesque – would prove key to its enduring popularity. For it is the visual beauty of the film that strikes home, allied with a powerful nostalgia on the part of both working- and middle-class viewers for a world that has now vanished completely: docks, streets, industries all now replaced by a new-build wilderness.

Much the same has been said of L.S. Lowry's paintings of Salford. In the words of Chris Waters: "Nostalgia for the world of mills and cobbled streets, and for the communities that were formed there, has been a ubiquitous feature of post-war British society … Their experience of modernity entailed a breakage of ties to the past, a visceral wiping out of whatever came before, and, consequently, the encouragement of forgetting. But in Britain in the 1950s, the pressure to forget was paralleled by a desire to remember, and it is no accident that urban renewal was accompanied by an interest in collecting those objects that could serve, in part, both to resurrect a lost past and reconnect people to it."[19]

The film of *A Taste of Honey* stands alongside Lowry's paintings as one of those objects symbolic of that distant past. Interestingly, Delaney herself has become enmeshed in the iconography. A series of photographs taken by the acclaimed American photographer Arnold Newman for the *Saturday Evening Post* in 1961 to publicise the film place her squarely in some of its most memorable settings. Best known for his iconic portraits of celebrities, Newman photographed such luminaries as the composer Igor Stravinsky, several presidents, and countless authors, actors, and artists, from Pablo Picasso to Truman Capote and Marilyn Monroe. Significantly, Newman is often credited as the first photographer to use environmental portraiture, in which the figure is portrayed in his or her chosen environment, rather than against a blank ground or studio backdrop.

So powerful were these images that they sparked off musician Morrissey's obsession with Delaney's work; indeed, he used one of them to embellish an album cover in the 1980s. However, although nostalgia accounts for Lowry's and Delaney's enduring popularity, it misses the essential point about the creation and ultimately the artistic worth of their work.

As it happens, Delaney would soon become increasingly concerned, both in her work and life, with the forces then at work destroying the world in which she had set her first and most memorable creation.

NOTES

1  Horne, in Welsh and Tibbetts, *Tony Richardson*.

2  Ibid.

3  http://www.webofstories.com/

4  *Spectator*, 22nd September 1961.

5  *Guardian*, 16th September 1961.

6  *The Times*, 13th September 1961.

7  *Daily Herald*, 15th September 1961.

8  John Russell Taylor, *Anger and After* (Pelican Books, 1963).

9  Terry Lovell, 'Landscapes and Stories in 1960s British Realism', *Screen*, 31, 4 (Winter 1990), p. 357.

10  John Hill, *Sex, Class and Realism* (BFI Publishing, 1986), p. 131.

11  Andrew Higson, 'Space, Place, Spectacle, Landscape and Townscape in the "Kitchen Sink" Film', *Screen*, 25, 4–5 (July–October 1984).

12  Ibid.

13  *Guardian*, 4th August 1976.

14  *Universities and New Left Review*, 8 (1961).

15  Nadine Holdsworth, *Joan Littlewood's Theatre* (Cambridge University Press, 2011).

16  Lovell, 'Landscapes and Stories' p. 357.

17  Adrian Page, *The Death of the Playwright? Modern British Drama and Literary Theory* (Palgrave Macmillan, 1992) includes Edward Esche, 'Shelagh Delaney's *A Taste of Honey* as Serious Text: A Semiotic Reading' (pp. 67–81).

18  *Daily Worker*, 16th October 1961.

19  Chris Waters 'Representations of Everyday Life: L. S. Lowry and the Landscape of Memory in Postwar Britain', *Representations*, 65 (Winter 1999), pp. 121–44.

# 14

## *Sweetly Sings the Donkey*

> Shelagh Delaney is a mythologist: all her backstreet frogs
> turn into fairy princesses or into reasonably demoniac kings
> … And, more overtly autobiographical, Delaney herself,
> transformed into sudden princess, but remembering the
> cobblestones.
>
> *The Times*, June 1968

The film of *A Taste of Honey* won awards and cemented Delaney's
position as a leading British writer, despite the failure of *Lion in Love*. By
now, she had a flat in Islington, London but was still writing in Salford
at the family home in Duchy Road. She had not, however, let *Lion in Love*
go. She believed in it, she felt it was a better play than *Honey*, and others
agreed. *Lion in Love* was awarded the Encyclopaedia Britannica Award
in 1962, and Delaney was presented with £500 and a silver medal by
Labour Party leader Hugh Gaitskell at the Savoy Hotel in December that
year. Perhaps buoyed by this, she pushed ahead with developing it for an
American audience. She was also working on a mysterious 'third play'
she had been dropping hints about for some time ("it's sexy and shocking
and set in an unidentified northern town").

It also became clear that she was looking to America rather than
home to place her new work. In April 1963 a small collection of semi-
autobiographical pieces called *Sweetly Sings the Donkey* was published
first in America in late 1963, and some months later, in March 1964, in
the UK.

In fact, parts of it had been published even earlier in various
American publications: *Harper's Bazaar* and *Cosmopolitan* ran extracts
in May and June 1963, as did the *Saturday Evening Post*, while the avant-
garde *Evergreen Review*, in its May/June issue, published one of the stories
(called 'Tom Riley') along with new work by Fyodor Abramov, Samuel
Beckett and the poet Federico García Lorca.

She also produced a short impressionistic piece about Blackpool in June 1963 for American *Vogue*, illustrated by an Henri Cartier-Bresson photograph. *Vogue* described her as, 'an entrancing young woman, six feet tall and thin, with blazing eyes ... writing for her is as natural as walking ... ' The article was entitled 'The English Fun-and-Chips Holiday Town' and would not have been out of place in *Sweetly Sings the Donkey*.

> Blackpool bawls its head off. Yours is a face favoured by fortune so chance you arm and throw a ball, punch a ball, roll a ball a ball a penny a ball, chance your aim ten shots a shilling every one a winner, bingo, all the sevens seventy seven, legs eleven, kelly's eye, blind twenty, bingo ...[1]

There would appear to have been a concerted push to establish Delaney as a prose writer to coincide with the reappearance of *Lion in Love* in New York in April 1963. Sadly, the off-Broadway production presented by Gerald Krone, Dorothy Olim and Irving Dorfman at One Sheridan Square on 25th April closed after just six performances. According to the *Village Voice* reviewer, their production was, 'lousy'. It was not, he concluded, all Delaney's fault, more a production disaster by director Ann Giudici who had cut numerous characters' speeches, given some of one character's lines to another, and transposed whole sections from one act to another. The reviewer felt he had no idea of the various characters' economic backgrounds, the relationships between them were undefined and there was no dramatic focus. "Confrontations became casual conversations; and the drama's points – which do exist – vanished into what looked like feckless time-killing." He concluded by suggesting that Delaney "should be furious", but in fact she had gone to New York to help rewrite sections of the play, and thus had to take some of the blame. *Lion in Love* was destined never to be produced and performed again.[2]

With nothing imminent on the horizon for Shelagh in terms of either the theatre or television, *Sweetly Sings the Donkey* would fill the breach. The small collection, her first foray into prose, is an impressionistic self-portrait moving chronologically from childhood to the present day via sketches of people she had known along the way, glimpses of her life as a writer, snatches of conversation with local Salford folk along with some trademark flights of the imagination. Though laced with her sharp wit and occasional downbeat self-deprecation, the overall impression given by the book is, as the *Salford Reporter* noted, a sad one, reflecting her own unhappiness with life in general.

In 'Sweetly Sings the Donkey', the longest piece, we are given an account

Photo: ©Mirrorpix

Photo: ©PA

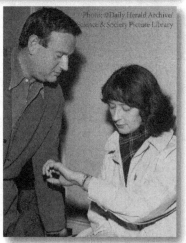

Photo: ©Daily Herald Archive/
Science & Society Picture Library

*Top:* Shelagh Delaney, Vanessa Redgrave, John Osborne and Doris Lessing. Trafalgar Square CND demonstration, September 1961.
*Bottom left:* Shelagh is delighted to receive her Encyclopaedia Britannica Award for *Lion in Love* from Labour Party leader Hugh Gaitskell, at the Savoy Hotel, 12th December 1962.
*Bottom right:* Shelagh with writer, producer, impresario Wolf Mankowitz, September 1960.

**Delaney and friends in the early 1960s.**

from Delaney's perspective of life in a convalescent home for children shortly after the Second World War. Much of it is taken up with descriptions of the nuns who ran the home: they are generally ill-informed and unkind apart from one younger nun whom Shelagh befriends and talks to. The government official who visits and inspects the children is pompous and aggressive. The other children suffer from illness, ignorance or disregard, and Shelagh's wit and bravado appear to shield her from an all-pervading sense of gloom. 'Tom Riley' is a story about a physically weak, over-mothered boy who dies at the hands of a cruel gang of his peers led by a bully. 'The Teacher' is, according to a reviewer, "Gothic in tone and denouement, [and] the chronicle of a despicable and sadistic teacher who flagrantly and self-righteously humiliates and tortures those pupils who, for one reason or another, do not please him. In the end, one of his victims avenges himself, after a particularly painful humiliation, by a deadly means that the book barely hints at."[3] 'My Uncle the Spy' is only a page long and is a small enigmatic conceit. 'Pavan for a Dead Prince' tells of a young miner – and we presume a teenage boyfriend of Shelagh's – who develops rheumatic fever, learns flamenco dancing while convalescing, exhausts himself dancing on recovery and dies – a romantically defiant piece, somewhat typical of her nature ("It is a romantic tragedy in which the narrator retains her cold, hard look at the things she loves without yielding an inch to conventional sentiment").[4] 'All about and to a Female Artist' is a collage of actual critical newspaper headlines written about Shelagh, plus letters she received after attaining fame, mostly either convoluted begging letters or long missives from would-be writers asking favours. 'Vodka and Small Pieces of Gold' is a travelogue piece about her trip to Poland as guest of the Writers' Union, consisting of various conversations she has whilst travelling and some topographical observations. Finally 'The White Bus' is a 'fantasy' about a trip around Salford on a local authority tourist bus … of which much more later.

Delaney and her agent were correct in favouring America for the book's début as it received practically no attention whatsoever on publication in the UK apart from her home-town review in early 1964. Of the American reviews, the *Village Voice*'s Julius Novick was the most penetrating (not surprising as Novick would later earn his Doctorate of Fine Arts from Yale with a dissertation on *Lion in Love*). Novick was unimpressed, calling the book "a grab-bag of bits and snatches, things and stuff, a collection of miscellany that for the most part might just as well have been left unpublished". He went further:

This book is shapeless and lumpy with unabsorbed matter. The lyricism of the plays is here reflected in a loose and hackneyed sentimentality. Her narrative style is abrupt and conversational: she hits off a good phrase now and again but she loses more on precision, polish and correct syntax than she can make up on spontaneity or zest. She underuses the comma and lets her sentences grow long and clumsy.[5]

Two pieces, however, he considered, were worth reading: 'All about and to a Female Artist' and 'Vodka and Small Pieces of Gold'. "And every once in a while throughout the book we get a glimpse of the buoyant, tough, splendidly cheeky spirit that illuminates the plays."[6]

Sean Callery, reviewing the book for the *Saturday Review*, noted an underlying melancholy pervading the pieces. "This last portion of the book suggests that Miss Delaney is not very enthusiastic about her new life [as a writer]. At any rate, she doesn't write very entertainingly about it. We eagerly await the fresh inspiration that seems certain to come to one who has written so well of the people she knew in the very near past."[7]

Back home, the *Salford Reporter* could see nothing objectionable in the collection, instead concentrating on the 'autobiographical' nature of it:

The first part of the book deals with childhood days in Lancashire and one is left with the impression that many of the incidents are based on the experiences the writer had herself. In the long account which gives the book its title, she deals with a seaside convalescent home run by nuns and the conversations give an illuminating view of the reactions to stern discipline by young girls. Underlying many of her stories are Miss Delaney's obvious dislike for bullies, her defence of the weaker people, and there is a sadness about some of her tales such as that concerning the delicate Tom Riley.

One thing the *Reporter* did note, however, was that the chapter, 'All about and to a Female Artist' contained comments about herself and her first play, included quite a number of begging letters which she received, "and some of it recalls the bitter correspondence in the *Reporter* and other newspapers which her first play produced."[8]

Despite the passage of time, that 'bitter correspondence' was continuing. Through editorials and letters the criticism of her and her work was unrelenting. In January 1963 she was being blamed by one correspondent for costing young people jobs in the city: "I hope that the jobless youngsters of today reflect sometimes that they might have been in secure jobs today had not the tarnished image of Salford created by Greenwood, Delaney and co. discouraged outsiders from setting up business here ..."[9]

In February 1963 the *Reporter* house journalist John Windsor, beneath a headline 'Speaking Up in Defence of Our Salford', said it was necessary "to stand up for Salford whenever one can in defence of it against the impression created by Shelagh Delaney". To that end, he revealed that the paper had organised an exhibition for the Hall Green Little Theatre of Birmingham which was producing *A Taste of Honey*. "The centrepiece was a compelling portrait of Shelagh Delaney which we were happy to lend to the organisers and it was accompanied by a wide range of scenes of Salford loaned by the Salford Libraries Dept." The paper had sent along a variety of photographs of the city and while there were photos of the 'dingiest parts', there were, "others of our good-class residential areas and of the magnificent new flats now reaching skywards, as well as other new buildings and delightful countryside ..."[10]

The play would soon be produced in Lincoln and the *Salford Reporter* display would follow it.

In September, a columnist reviewed a BBC Home Service radio talk entitled 'Salford in Focus' and commented that listeners would, "forget the fictional picture of Salford as a place of slums and squalor which is a hang-over from the bad old days. It bears no resemblance to the present position and it is an insult to the City Council which has already poured a score of a million pounds into redevelopment and has £14m more in the pipeline at the present moment."[11]

And some months later a correspondent wrote all the way from Canada about a performance of *A Taste of Honey* at a drama festival at Charlottetown, Prince Edward Island: "It makes me very angry to see such slurs cast on the city of Salford. The author, I believe, has done irreparable damage to the name of Salford. Nothing can be done about it now I suppose but I do wish some of the stories could be refuted." How could a girl know so much of the dock area? he asked. They were not a safe place for girls, what with "sailors looking for a good time". He concluded: "She must have a bitter taste in her mouth to besmirch the city which gave her birth and in which her family still reside, I believe."[12]

By the time this letter had been printed, however, Delaney's 'family life' had moved irrevocably south. On 3rd April, on the front page of the *Reporter*, it was announced beneath a headline, 'Ma Shelagh Keeps Them All Guessing', that Delaney had given birth to a daughter in a nursing home a month previously and that her mother had travelled to London to stay with her.

Tellingly, the *Reporter* article was accompanied by a picture of Delaney (left hand unadorned by a ring) positioned immediately below two large pictures of local Salford girls and one of a young man receiving the traditional 'dressing' by workmates – a custom whereby anyone about to be married is garlanded in tatters and motley. "What everyone wanted to know", the report on Delaney's new-born child began, "was when she was married and to whom."[13]

Delaney was not telling, and certainly not the *Salford Reporter*. The *Daily Mail* reporter was also given short shrift when appearing on her doorstep and so searched further afield for quotes. He found an unnamed friend who commented, "It is typical of Shelagh to make an announcement on April Fool's Day and then refuse to make any further comment. She enjoys doing that kind of thing."[14]

The *Daily Express* was more fortunate, however: "A happy Shelagh Delaney came to the door of her fourth floor flat behind St Pancras Town Hall last night to tell me about her daughter. We had to whisper because the baby was sleeping. 'She's a lovely little girl,' said Shelagh. 'It's a pity I can't let you see her but you might wake her up.' Widowed Mrs Delaney who has been with her since the baby was born in a Paddington nursing home, tiptoed in the background."

Delaney was, according to the reporter, already having to combine the obligations of a mother and a writer. "Just now I am struggling with a new play and I've got to meet a deadline in a fortnight," she said. Its theme? "There's a lot of me mixed up in it."

As for the mystery of the missing father, the *Express* could only speculate. There was a secret engagement to an American, reported the previous year, and there was a "heavy band of gold" on her wedding finger, but Delaney was saying nothing more.

Back in Manchester, her brother Jo was tracked down and commented, "She always said her private life was going to be kept very private."[15] He was right. This was to be the last time for more than a decade that Shelagh Delaney would talk to the outside world about anything at all.

NOTES

1  American *Vogue* (June 1963).
2  *Village Voice*, 2nd May 1963.
3  Sean Callery in *Saturday Review* (July/August 1963).
4  Ibid.
5  *Village Voice*, 12th September 1963.
6  Ibid.
7  Sean Callery in *Saturday Review* (July/August 1963).
8  *SCR*, 26th March 1964.
9  *SCR*, 25th January 1963.
10  *SCR*, 15th February 1963.
11  *SCR*, 6th September 1963.
12  *SCR*, 10th July 1964.
13  *SCR*, 3rd April 1964.
14  *Daily Mail*, 2nd April 1964.
15  *Daily Express*, 2nd April 1964.

# 15

## See Your City

You're very unpopular with some people in this city you
know. But I'm more tolerant. Ever since I saw you on
television I've been wanting to meet you.

**Mayor to the Girl on the White Bus,**
in *Sweetly Sings the Donkey*, 1963

Though Shelagh had received considerable criticism from a variety of
Salfordian sources, she had never responded other than to make the
occasional sharp remark to anyone from the *Salford Reporter* having the
temerity to arrive on her Duchy Road doorstep. With the filming of *The
White Bus*, however, based on the short sketch that had concluded her
*Sweetly Sings the Donkey* collection, she moved on to the attack.

The idea for filming the piece had come in June, four months after
the birth of her daughter and was floated by one of her constant
champions, Oscar Lewenstein. Along with his work in the theatre at the
Royal Court, Lewenstein had found himself drawn into the revival of
British film production as a director of John Osborne and Tony
Richardson's film company Woodfall Films, working on *A Taste of
Honey* (1961) and *The Loneliness of the Long Distance Runner* (1962), as
associate producer on *Tom Jones* (1962) and as producer on *The Girl with
Green Eyes* (1964) and *The Knack* (1965).

In June 1964 he proposed a three-film project for Woodfall Films that
aimed to reunite three leading figures of the Free Cinema movement:
Karel Reisz, Tony Richardson and Lindsay Anderson. Anderson recalled:
"[Lewenstein] wanted to bring three directors of original personality
together, to make a film in three segments. His first idea was that these
pictures should not be related in any way, except that each should
represent the free choice of its director."[1]

Lewenstein later suggested they use Delaney's book of short stories as
a common source of inspiration. Anderson was immediately enthusiastic:

"I liked the story ['The White Bus'] and I liked Shelagh, and I agreed to do it. Tony Richardson hit on another story from the same collection ..." Reisz, however, dropped out, to be replaced by director Peter Brook. The trilogy, to be titled *Red White and Zero*, would eventually not turn out to be what Lewenstein had envisaged. Nevertheless, in March 1965, Anderson began working with Shelagh on a script.

Like his co-Free Cinema collaborator Tony Richardson, Anderson had made film documentaries in the 1950s but from 1957 to about 1962 he'd worked exclusively in the theatre, the Royal Court in particular. Here he directed many new and challenging pieces of theatre including *Serjeant Musgrave's Dance* by John Arden in 1959 and *Billy Liar* by Keith Waterhouse in 1960. He'd forgone film-making apart from the critically successful *This Sporting Life*, largely because, as he put it, "I wasn't interested in making sponsored films. It's almost impossible to find financing for creative work."[2] Lewenstein now gave him all the freedom he wanted.

He was immediately apprised of the genesis of 'The White Bus' and its meaning for Shelagh. "Shelagh's story had been essentially personal and subjective. When her play, *A Taste of Honey*, had been produced in London, she found herself reviled and attacked in her home town, the North Country city of Salford. Puritanical tradition was still strong in the North, and Shelagh's frankness with speech and emotion shocked the local dignitaries, who also felt that she had presented an unworthy picture of the city to the world. Outraged statements were made in speeches and in newspapers, and the local Council even went so far as to sponsor tours of Salford in special buses, to show off the beauties and advantages of the locality."[3]

Although not intended to be a factual account, the 'White Bus' story describes the author's return to Salford on a train carrying football supporters, ostensibly having been to see an England international. The drinking and singing has the effect of condensing time, and they arrive in Manchester almost at midnight, which contributes to the overall sense of unreality about the trip; indeed, the whole piece feels like an extended dream.

The supporters catch their buses and, left alone, Delaney awaits hers outside the station in the bitter cold. She watches a procession of nuns on their way to Lourdes and she becomes again the small girl in the story at the beginning of the collection, teasing the religious with sly questions. With no explanation, a White Bus appears full of passengers, and the Mayor (of Salford?) suggests Delaney joins them. He and the mace-bearer are wearing full regalia, and he immediately launches into a personal statement about how he rose from nothing to be in his present position. The tour he announces is to present the city "as it really is", its people and its achievements. Problems are acknowledged. There is unemployment, exploitation. There are social ills – but the tour will demonstrate what a fine race of people Salfordians are. He then mentions various cultural events in the offing, including the opening of the city's first professional repertory theatre. It had originally been an old theatre which was then used as a warehouse and since bought by himself. He intends to relaunch it as a theatre and, although he has been warned he will lose money, he remains confident.

The tour starts and the Mayor sits down next to Delaney and asks her, "Aren't you that girl – the one who writes?" Yes, she says, and he berates her for her choice of topics, "unmarried mothers and things and homosexuals ... you've given us a bad reputation in the eyes of the country, you know." He asks her whether she's made a lot of money, tells her how much he is worth and then suggests they have dinner together so that he can give her advice. He suggests his life would make the subject for a good book and hopes he isn't being too paternal. Delaney thanks him and asks him to take his hand off her knee.

The tour guide then takes over, announcing places of interest as they move along. They leave the industrial part of town and reach a park built by a 19th-century social reformer. Next comes the Hope Hospital, (originally a workhouse) and after that a large building which houses the school Delaney had once attended and which had originally been the home of an industrial magnate. The guide extols the virtues of similar men who made money but also built rest homes for workers, but the detailing of their philanthropy is written in self-consciously 'ironic' mode designed to undermine their virtues. In case we miss the point, the mace-bearer slips in scurrilous *sotto voce* comments ("got a good screw out of the industrial revolution ... Bloody Josiah!").

When they reach the Central Library the Mayor begins a long rant about the "disgusting books" which are housed there ("proselytising tracts for homosexual practices") some of which were written by a clergyman who was sentenced to ten years "for perversion". Thence to the Gas Works and to the Council Welfare Departments where once again 19th-century reformers are praised for their work, especially the Ladies' Sanitary Reform Association ("the poor are most grateful for the agents' visits", the guide informs everyone).

Children's Homes, Old People's Homes, the Zoo – all are passed by and they reach a café for a break. Inside, the mace-bearer asks Delaney to open her mouth and he places a biscuit on her tongue and mutters loudly in Italian. Delaney then feels afraid and flees, feeling increasingly queasy following the drinking she had done on the train.

She reaches a graveyard, and an old man thinks she is crying for a dead person. She vomits and then looks down at the gravestone of a twenty-year-old man called Ernest Titterington who died in 1854. She ponders on his youth, then walks home, passing through an area of the city that is being demolished.

She sees smashed homes, their interiors revealed to the light while, "All around this deserted place the new city sheered up higher then ever before." She passes a courting couple whose banter sounds very like Jo and Jimmy from *A Taste of Honey* ("Then why don't you? [want to kiss me]" "Because I feel so daft").

Finally she passes a closing chip shop where the old couple inside are talking, the woman pressing her husband to clean up before they go to bed. The man starts to work; "and I went away, murmuring," the story concludes.

By juxtaposing the bigotry, philistinism and 'boosterism' of a municipal politician with the brutal past and present of the town over which he rules, Delaney had sought, through exaggeration and gentle parody, to expose some of the pomposity and hypocrisy of local Salford dignitaries.

In fact, she had invented very little of the text. Certain sections of the speech delivered by the Mayor were lifted from letters and statements appearing in the local newspaper; whilst the attack on dirty books in the local libraries came almost verbatim from one reader's letter.[4] There was also the fact that she had made an attempt to establish a community theatre similar to the one mentioned by the Mayor, only to be thwarted by politicians just like him.

Most significant of all, however, the White Bus itself was no fantasy. In 1961 the city had employed Granada TV's first public relations man, J.P. Phoenix, ostensibly to present a 'positive' image of the city, but also to counter the 'negative' publicity Delaney herself had generated. Phoenix's firm, Protel, had come up with the original touring buses. Simultaneously, Granada TV interviewed Alderman Hamburger (one of Delaney's most vehement critics), who'd lauded the town and its achievements and seen the tours and the publicity as a chance to 'sell' the city. The lady Mayor had also toured the city along with *Coronation Street* actress Pat Phoenix – ironically she played a very Delaney-type character in the soap called Elsie Tanner – and thousands had turned out to watch.

For a charge of 1s. 6d for adults, and 9d for children, the buses ferried interested citizens around local sites of interest, including the post-war housing developments ("but the premises will not be open to the public"), the new municipal cleansing department, the Art Gallery, the Royal College of Advanced Technology, the new police headquarters (where there were police dog displays and the police band played) plus the new Fire Brigade headquarters. Guides gave information about the places en route. Thus, everything that would appear in *The White Bus* had already happened in real life. It's hard to tell who exactly went on the tours but they were clearly a novelty.

The piece was so clearly a personal statement that for a time Anderson wanted Shelagh herself to play the Girl. Shelagh declined. The call thus went out for someone to play the central role in similar fashion to the search for *A Taste of Honey*'s Jo that had resulted in Rita Tushingham appearing from obscurity. The *Salford Reporter* announced that the company was looking for a double, "no mean problem because she is very tall and has a highly individual cast of feature".[5] Artist Harold Riley had been asked to keep his eyes open in Salford for likely candidates.

In the event, it was Shelagh who suggested the actress Patricia Healey. Healey had earlier appeared in *Lion in Love*, had been working for two years in the Midland Theatre Company in Coventry and had just finished filming a play, *A Piece of Resistance*, for television. Though born in Manchester, she'd never set foot in Salford before. Anderson commented, "Some people have remarked that Patsy looks a bit like Shelagh in the film; I suppose their hair was similar but that wasn't the reason I chose her."[6]

Others in the cast were various experienced but unknown film and TV actors. John Sharp played the town crier carrying the mace and, in smaller roles, newcomers Stephen Moore, Barry Evans and Anthony Hopkins. For the role of the Mayor, however, Anderson chose Arthur Lowe, by then a veteran of the cinema and well known on TV as the draper/lay preacher Leonard Swindley in Coronation Street. He'd already featured in Anderson's earlier film *This Sporting Life*, and within a year would become even more of a national star when taking on the role of Captain Mainwaring of *Dad's Army*. In fact, his performance in *The White Bus* uncannily prefigured Mainwaring: pompous, overbearing, vain and oddly vulnerable.

Anderson and Delaney collaborated closely on the basic script, but as the project advanced it was clear that the natural *auteur* in Anderson was emerging, just as Tony Richardson had gradually taken control of the film of *A Taste of Honey*. Anderson played various pieces of music that he thought might work in the picture to Shelagh, and after showing her an earlier documentary film he'd made, he noted, "She understood: and we chatted about the style – the beginning – the end – the crucial mid-point where the bus arrives and a sort of realism (however personal) that changes into a sort of fantasy (however concrete)." He revealed an impatience, however, with discussing a set script, and noted that their discussion "remained vague".[7]

Anderson began shooting on 18th October 1965 at a variety of locations including Manchester city centre, Manchester Town Hall, the Central Library and Piccadilly Gardens, while Manchester Piccadilly and Manchester Central stations were also used. The filming then moved to Salford and featured the high-rise Kersal Flats estate, factories in Trafford Park, notably the Metropolitan-Vickers works where Shelagh had once been employed. There were both the exterior and interior shots taken of her old school Pendleton High School for Girls, as well as extended sequences in Buile Hill Park where she'd spent many hours with Harold Riley, drinking coffee and listening to the jukebox.

The *Salford Reporter* soon got wind of the proceedings and on 22nd October beneath a headline 'Another Slur on Salford's Good Name' it insisted that, "the poorer parts of the city are the exception rather than the rule," and went on to criticise what it termed, "deliberately slanted" images of Salford, suggesting that television was the worst offender, *Coronation Street* in particular. The writer also defended people in poorer housing, saying the interiors were "neat and clean as a proverbial new pin … even if without Hollywood-style toilet suites". Where *The White Bus* was concerned, it declared, "There have been assurances that it will not be a 'knock' against the city."[8]

Those assurances, wherever they had originated, would not be honoured.

NOTES

1　Lindsay Anderson, programme notes for Gary Sweet's showing of *The White Bus* (3 December 1979).
2　'Class Theatre, Class Film: An Interview with Lindsay Anderson', *Tulane Drama Review*, 11, 1 (Autumn 1966), pp. 122–9.
3　Lindsay Anderson, programme notes.
4　*SCR*, 15th June 1962.
5　*SCR*, 17th September 1965.
6　*Never Apologise: The Collected Writings of Lindsay Anderson*, ed. Paul Ryan (Plexus, 2004).
7　Lindsay Anderson, *Diaries*, ed. Paul Sutton (Methuen 2006).
8　*SCR*, 22nd October 1965.

# 16

## *Red, White ... and Zero*

[The White Bus] succeeds remarkably well in creating a
world at once both fantastic and realistic, a picture of life
in a northern city observed with love, with alarm, with
nostalgia and often with a wicked sense of fun by its wide-
eyed heroine from the dubious vantage point of a fantas-
ticated "See Your City" bus tour.

John Russell Taylor, *The Times,* July 1968

Like Tony Richardson before him, Anderson would be fascinated by what
he termed the "usual stimulating awful marvellous Northern urban
landscape". that he found when venturing forth into Salford. Anderson
had seen Ken Russell's *Monitor* documentary about Delaney and was
inspired by it. Thus, the film would be shot predominantly in black and
white although, from an early stage, Anderson was contemplating also
using colour: "The non-naturalism of *The White Bus* is to me one of its
most attractive qualities: the freedom to experiment in terms of sound
and of image. While we were working on the script the idea came of
injecting short bursts of colour into an otherwise black-and-white
narrative – the obverse of *If* ... [Anderson's next major film, where a
colour film was interspersed with sequences in monochrome]. Clearly
what I was groping towards was a style that would be poetically
expressive rather than naturalistically faithful to 'real life.'"[1]

From a philosophical point of view, it soon became clear that the
project would be an extension of Anderson's abiding social and political
preoccupations. He was a fierce critic of modern society: the
unaccountability of medical science, the corruption in public life, the
corrosion of values in mass entertainment – these and other issues he
felt obliged to tackle in his work. He felt that both film and the theatre
were failing to tackle the problems of modern society. Despite the recent
establishment of the National Theatre and the work of a small group of

experimental film-makers, he felt that "The general climate is just as conformist as it ever was, but now it is expressed in shinier terms. The premium on success in Britain has become much stronger. It's no longer fashionable to be an outsider or to retain certain personal standards of integrity. This used to be at least respectable. Not any more." He went on: "We're living in a society which is making a determined refusal to face reality. Britain today is really a sort of madhouse. The whole life of the nation is built on the most absurd paradox. You've only to switch on the television set and one minute you'll be seeing a politician addressing the nation on the need to face realities and devote ourselves to genuine productivity; the next moment you get a series of commercials bludgeoning you into trying to buy a pile of absolutely useless or trivial products."[2]

He was not a *political* radical, however. In 1959 he had collaborated on the film *March to Aldermaston* about the nascent CND movement during which the possibility of a 'Popular Front' of political and creative people coming together had been mooted. That aspiration had, according to Anderson, failed: "I don't regret having tried to join a New Left because it would have been very nice if it had amounted to anything. Writers, film-makers, politicians joining together etc." But the politicians, he felt, had only been interested in art that was 'propagandist'. "If our work was socially acceptable then okay – otherwise they just became the new generation of politicians."[3]

More radical than Richardson, his development of Delaney's story would be harsher, more satirical, where Richardson's vision had been predominantly lyrical and sentimental. From his comments regarding the development of the idea, it's also clear that he felt he was taking Delaney's work onto another level: "Shelagh and I worked closely together to produce a script which derived closely from the original story, but which went a good way beyond it … A lot of *The White Bus* was not scripted, and I don't think it could have been really."[4] He also underlined the fact that making a film was more than simply translating the writer's ideas onto celluloid. He explained: "I think that a writer is more likely to be satisfied as a playwright than as a script writer because a film script undergoes a more profound and radical transformation. In my experience, a writer is apt to find the film made from his script an agonizing experience. Even if the film is a good one, it is agonizing to see something which he has imagined turned into something else. He is apt to feel a gross sense of deprivation, a helplessness."[5]

How Delaney felt when watching her short sketch being turned into a movie is difficult to say but, unlike when *A Taste of Honey* was being filmed, she was on the spot watching as the camera crew went about their business.

Anderson noted: "I liked Shelagh very much; we got along well, although, once shooting was under way, she didn't say much. She was there, but she didn't really participate. After a script adjustment, I might say to Shelagh, 'Is that all right?' and she'd say, 'Yes.' I think she felt that the actual making of the film wasn't really her bag."[6]

Anderson, meanwhile, was constantly reacting to what he saw in similar fashion to Richardson, seizing opportunities as they presented themselves rather than planning things beforehand. There was, for instance, a scene in the Salford Museum, where he shot close-ups of stuffed animals and juxtaposed them with the faces of the actors. "Shelagh wouldn't go into the museum, so she never saw the animals or put them in the script. But I saw them when we were going around the museum, and decided to improvise the scene."[7]

Shelagh would certainly have enjoyed the sense of mischief accompanying the making of *The White Bus* – that the city fathers and those in authority would not have approved of what was going on had they but known. This would be her revenge, perhaps, after years of constant denigration. Anderson admitted later that he and the film crew had found it necessary to dupe people whose properties they wanted to film, concealing their true intentions behind the pretence that they were shooting a documentary. Having, for example, investigated the Town Hall, "the most superb neo-Gothic building you can imagine", they sought permission for shooting, "sitting there with the butter melting in our mouths, lying like dogs, and feeling like assassins with knives under our cloaks".[8]

Even Shelagh's old school had been taken in. Her old headmistress, Miss Pearson, oversaw one scene when the girls sang in the school hall. Miss Pearson even had a part, greeting the 'Mayor', played by Arthur Lowe.

Just as with *Honey*, however, ordinary local people found themselves being called into the action and the *cinéma vérité* aspect was very much to the fore. In November the *Reporter* gave details of the hectic week of Mrs Veronica Gardener and her daughter Patricia of Northallerton Street, Lower Kersal:

They are keen supporters of Manchester United and down at the supporters' club a month ago they were asked along with other members if they would act as extras for the film. The first shots were taken at Piccadilly Station when as a crowd of football fans coming back from a match they are all supposed to get off a train and run up and down the platform. The first person to get off the train and into the film was Patricia with Mum following closely behind. Mrs Gardener has her moment of triumph too for she was filmed walking up the platform with the Manchester United mascot. Both mother and daughter were in the 'Pilgrimage to Lourdes' scene.[9]

The film itself opens with a boy on a boat going down the Thames holding a dove. It then cuts to office worker (Patsy Healey aka Delaney) ending her boring working day and leaving London. From the start, Anderson employed disorientating changes of register to distance the audience from the comfort and security of thinking they were watching a mainstream film with a 'coherent' storyline. As soon as the office empties, the film cuts to Healey's body dangling above the desks, hanging from a rope. The cleaners below carry on as if nothing untoward has happened and seconds later we see the girl taking her coat and leaving. Had she been fantasising about suicide? There are no clues. Likewise, when she leaves the building, it isn't, as we have assumed, late at night but a Saturday morning, and the girl watches a young man listening to a football match on a transistor radio, which is where Delaney's original story starts.

As she makes her way to the railway station, she encounters a well-dressed, bowler-hatted City gent who tries to pick her up. Although he claims he isn't class-conscious, his chatter is filled with references to upper-class ideas and leisure pursuits; the girl says nothing. He chases after her until finally, aboard her train, she leans out and says to him that she "will write". The young man's dialogue was apparently suggested by Shelagh's brother, who was also on hand during scripting and filming.

She then travels north, as in the written story, with a group of Manchester United football fans who drink and sing and engage her in their largely innocent, good-natured revelries. When they arrive in Manchester, the supporters hurry away, and she is left alone. As she leaves the station platform, she encounters a procession of people we assume (if we are familiar with her story) are on their way to Lourdes: they are blind and lame, and someone being wheeled along by nuns is in an iron lung.

She leaves the station and finds herself in a deserted city; she looks up

151

*Top left:* Original Salford Council advert, 28th July 1961.
*Top right:* Lindsay Anderson and Shelagh Delaney on location in Buile Hill Park Salford, October 1965.
*Bottom:* The fictional bus setting out on its satirical mystery tour, October 1965.

**The White Bus.**

at various Victorian statues (as in *A Taste of Honey*), then watches as two men chase a frantic woman and bundle her into a car before driving off at speed. An athlete runs past, she wanders past a wholesale butcher's with carcasses hanging before the film switches briefly to colour. She gazes out at a half-demolished church and a desolate landscape that once boasted terraced housing. She is now at a bus stop and the White Bus appears.

It is full of guests and led by Arthur Lowe's Mayor. There is a female tour guide, who recites a plethora of facts and figures about the city in an expressionless voice. The travellers will be seeing, "Places old and new, past and present and of our heritage", plus "meeting people noted for their warmth and friendliness". Leading the tour, the Mayor promotes the city's progress and shows off its finest achievements, doing so with a great deal of self-satisfaction and without a hint of irony. He recounts how he was born in the city and is proud of it, and proud that he has worked his way up.

Those on the bus are a peculiar mix of middle-aged ladies wearing floral hats and also people wearing their national dress: Japanese kimonos, Indian kaftans. All are given walkie-talkie sets and, as the bus trip proceeds, the film switches in and out of colour with no apparent logic. They view real industrial scenes, a working factory, they pass through a refrigerated meat warehouse full of carcasses, then into a steel mill where red-hot metal is turned into engine parts and machine tools.

The Mayor then declares: "Science has liberated the worker but he needs to be educated to take advantage of it." The party is shown round a council-run college where various pursuits are being demonstrated in pottery, baking and sewing classes. Finally, and quite bizarrely, they listen to a young Anthony Hopkins singing a Brecht song in the public library.

As the bus drives past new blocks of residential high-rise flats the tour guide outlines the city's achievements ("its finest") in clearing slums and creating new communities. Though admitting that such estates are unpopular, she explains, "We are gradually breaking down this resistance." There follows a visit to a local park where Manet and Fragonard paintings come to life, enacted by local people recruited on the day.

Throughout the film, Healey has hardly a line of dialogue to speak. Instead, she stares almost expressionlessly at whatever passes in front of her: the sterile housing estates, the factories, libraries, museums and Delaney's own school, where Healey joins the girls in singing Vaughan Williams's 'Let Us Now Praise Famous Men'.

The sequences veer from the factual to the surreal. The Mayor intones lines from the Bible (Proverbs 4:7) when entering the city library: "Wisdom is the principal thing; therefore get wisdom: and with thy getting, get understanding," but he immediately undermines this noble thought by launching into an extended reactionary rant to the librarian standing beside him about the "disgusting books" in the same library.

On the tour of the City Museum, the dignitaries and worthies are shown peering closely at the stuffed birds and mammals on display with which they are compared by intercut juxtaposition or framed proximity. A bowler-hatted gentleman stops beside the skeleton of an ape while a genteel elderly lady hisses aggressively at a small stuffed monkey on a branch.

Suddenly the film cuts to a woman screaming and running through a bomb-devastated landscape accompanied by machine-gun fire. It is, in fact, a Civil Defence demonstration complete with sirens and realistic explosions and a tannoy-relayed explanation of the role of civil defence. There's a sense here that this is Delaney's childhood in the blitz being re-enacted before her, and it's not long before she rises and leaves the special stand in which she and the bus passengers have been sitting. As she leaves, we see that they have been transformed into lifeless dummies.

She walks though the smoke-ridden scene with firemen hosing down blazing buildings and into a tranquil playground where children are playing. Seen from above, it looks very like the Ordsall district where she grew up, with old-style back-to-back houses and smoky chimneys. The Girl wanders along cobbled streets at dusk, past a courting couple in the alleyway, peeks into windows where she sees a girl playing a piano and an old man being shaved by his wife with the street-lights glowing in the mist and murk.

She ends up in a chip shop where an elderly couple are clearing up. Their final lines of dialogue are taken directly from Delaney's short story. The man suggests they leave the tidying-up until the next day, but his wife recites a repetitive mantra as she sweeps up: "If we don't do Saturday's work till Sunday, we won't do Sunday's work till Monday, we won't do Monday's work till Tuesday, we won't do Tuesday's work till Wednesday, we won't do Wednesday's work till Thursday, we won't do Thursday's work till Friday, we won't do Friday's work till Saturday and we'll never catch Saturday's work again." As Healey finishes her fish and chips, the film fades and ends.

The look of the film is quite striking. Shot by Czech cinematographer Miroslav Ondříček, who'd earlier worked on Miloš Forman's *A Blonde in Love* and would remain with Anderson for both *If ...* and *O Lucky Man!*, the Salford landscapes have an almost post-apocalyptic, abandoned feeling to them at times, while the accompanying music by Misha Donat (he would write music for another Delaney film, *Charlie Bubbles*), employing banjos and accordions, xylophones and a honky-tonk piano creates a swirling fairground feel, rather like the soundtrack to a French New Wave film.

At the time producer Oscar Lewenstein failed to grasp many of the the cultural references and Anderson's film remains difficult to appreciate fully today for the average audience. In fact, *The White Bus* can appear as bizarre, obscure and not a little confusing. Its sudden disorientating changes of mood and pace and place; the surreal twists; the switching between black-and-white and colour – all can be justified in terms of Anderson's progress as a director, but they have the overall effect of taking us further and further away from Delaney's original intentions. Looking back from 1979, Anderson distinguished in greater detail between the print and screen versions:

"[The] fantastic elements [of the published story] were preserved in our treatment, but I think that the objective or satirical side of the story was probably strengthened. In its eventual form in fact, *The White Bus* is more of a mini-epic than a fantasy, and looking back on it in this way I can see clearly how it lay at the beginning of an artistic journey which was to lead me forward to *If ...* and to *O Lucky Man!*"[10]

Anderson was paid for his work in February 1966 and the finished film, after much editing, was screened privately in April (Prague), June (London) and September (Venice). As might have been foreseen, the Delaney 'trilogy' of which it was to be a part never materialised. Anderson later explained: "When Tony Richardson and Peter Brook saw *The White Bus* they immediately decided that they should try and make something more remarkable and they jettisoned Shelagh Delaney. The subjects they chose were not good, and when all three films were together under the blanket title *Red, White and Zero* the whole thing made no sense. I certainly don't blame United Artists for not distributing it."[11]

*The White Bus* was placed on a shelf by the same United Artists and left there. Apart from a brief release in the Paris Pullman cinema in London in July 1968, a late-night transmission by BBC Television in 1981 and occasional film society screenings, it has remained unseen.

For Delaney, the film's subsequent burial must have been a deep disappointment, although it is probably just as well for Salford that the film was never shown outside the confines of London art houses. Though she never openly criticised her ungrateful home town in her work, the

*White Bus* film would have dealt a wounding blow had those in positions of authority grasped its nature. The original bus tours upon which the story is based had been the city's riposte to Shelagh herself and to what her critics felt her work represented. The Anderson film had turned their purpose upside down and mocked them, ridiculed the intentions of their creators and rejected much of what the city's spokespersons claimed was good for its own people.

For the major twist in Anderson's film was that the bus passengers were not ordinary working-class people – as those who had taken the original tours might have been. Owen Hatherley comments: "In the film, it's as if Manchester's middle classes collectively decided that they wanted to know how the other half lived, and descended upon it to find out. Thus, they were being taken around precisely those parts of the city they wouldn't normally see – the districts they don't travel through, the factories they won't work in, the flats they won't live in. Looked at that way, it's darker – a brief holiday in others' lives, where you can stop, see that something is being done and return to a safer, richer place. That's the contemporary resonance right there: the urban explorers, the consumers of ruin porn, the psychogeographers, all encourage us to see our city anew, but can so easily, in the process, transform these forgotten places into a more recherché form of tourism."[12]

That the film had a fictional Shelagh Delaney in their midst, singing in her old school, wandering about its municipal buildings, even reprimanding the Mayor for touching her knee would only have inflamed the city fathers further.

Despite its relative failure, the influence of *The White Bus* can be seen in another 'road movie' that attracted much more attention just a year later. The Beatles' Paul McCartney would have seen Anderson's film on the underground film circuit. *Magical Mystery Tour* was conceived by him in mid-1967: unscripted and shot on the basis of a mostly handwritten collection of ideas, sketches and situations, it has something of the same quirky British unreality of *The White Bus* to it.

In fact, McCartney had already looked to Delaney for inspiration in his work. Some years earlier he had taken the theme tune written for the 1960 Broadway version of *A Taste of Honey* by Bobby Scott and Ric Marlow and, with slight alterations to the lyrics, turned it into a popular Beatles number. He now he took a line from *A Taste of Honey* and used it to write one of the *Magical Mystery Tour*'s most popular numbers, 'Your Mother Should Know'.

NOTES

1 Lindsay Anderson, programme notes for Gary Sweet's showing of *The White Bus* (3rd December 1979).

2 Paul Gray and Kelly Morris, 'Class Theatre, Class Film: An Interview with Lindsay Anderson', *The Tulane Drama Review*, 11, 1 (Autumn, 1966), pp. 122–9.

3 Archer Robin et al. (eds.), *Out of Apathy: Voice of the New Left Thirty Years On* (Verso, 1989).

4 Anderson, programme notes.

5 Gray and Morris, 'Class Theatre, Class Film'.

6 Anderson, *Never Apologise*.

7 Ibid.

8 Anderson, *Diaries*.

9 *SCR*, 12th November 1965.

10 Anderson, programme notes.

11 Anderson, *Never Apologise*.

12 Owen Hatherley, 'When Urban Trawls Become Ruin Porn', *Building Design* (April 2012), p. 7.

# 17

# Charlie Bubbles

"In the end, he goes up in a balloon and cuts the rope. He sails up into the big blue sky. That stayed in my head, that scene," said George. "Pure escape, turning your back on it all, on the world."

**George Best,** *The Observer,* **November 2005**

Shelagh had little time to mourn the failure of *The White Bus*. Indeed, while Anderson's film was toiling through its post-production stages, ultimately to end in obscurity, she was already working on her next film project.

Albert Finney and Shelagh Delaney were born within a couple of years of one another and lived in the immediate post-Second World War years no more than a mile apart, he in Seedley, she in Brindle Heath, separated by Buile Hill Park. Finney's father and his grandfather before him were both bookmakers, both going by the name of 'Honest' Albert. The first family home in Romney Street, Pendleton, was damaged by German bombs while six-year-old Albert lay in an air raid shelter. The family then moved to Gore Crescent. "It seemed posh," he said in an interview. "It affected my mother, Alice, because she'd gone up-market and suddenly was aware of the neighbours in a way she hadn't been before. One was affected by that change in that you didn't live on the streets in the same way."[1] Unlike Shelagh, Finney passed the eleven-plus exam and attended Salford Grammar School but his approach to academic study was similar to hers. "I was in the top grade when I went to the grammar school but that didn't last because I wouldn't work. I hated homework. I thought it was an imposition on my childhood," he had said.[2]

Though he failed all but one of his O-Level exams two years running, the talent Finney had shown led to him being kept down in the fifth form for a further year, where he played Falstaff in *Henry IV Part I* and the

Emperor Jones in the same productions as Shelagh Delaney's great friend, Harold Riley. His head teacher then recommended the teenager to go to RADA.

Finney would express himself in identical terms to Shelagh where his career was concerned. "I was dead lucky. I've always been lucky," he told a reporter in 2012. "I got a job at Birmingham Rep while I was still at RADA. It was one of the leading reps in the country."[3] That was in 1958, the same year Delaney's *A Taste of Honey* was produced at Stratford East. The two ex-Salfordians then circled one another professionally for the next few years still without actually meeting. As *Honey* moved into the West End, Finney was appearing on television as a patient in *Emergency Ward 10*. He simultaneously made his West End début in Charles Laughton's production of *The Party* by Jane Arden before commencing a series of plays and films that would propel him into the limelight. He essayed such roles as Cassio in *Othello* (directed by Tony Richardson, with Paul Robeson playing the title character), Lysander in *A Midsummer Night's Dream* (again working with Charles Laughton), and understudied another English stage legend, Laurence Olivier, in *Coriolanus*, receiving critical acclaim when he briefly took over the lead.

While he continued to triumph on the English stage (in such plays as *The Lily White Boys* and, especially, *Billy Liar* with the Royal Court Theatre), feature films beckoned, with 1960 becoming a watershed year for him. He played the small part of Archie Rice's son, Mick Rice, in *The Entertainer* (reuniting him with director Tony Richardson once again), then won critical acclaim and enormous success as the brawling, non-conforming factory worker, Arthur Seaton, in Karel Reisz's *Saturday Night and Sunday Morning*. For only his second motion picture role, Finney's performance earned him two BAFTA nominations (one as Best Actor, the other for Most Promising Newcomer), as well as the Best Actor prize from the National Board of Review.

That particular role led Tony Richardson to cast him as Henry Fielding's rakish, picaresque, bawdy Tom Jones in the film of the same name in 1963. The film won four Oscars, including Best Picture, and earned Finney the first of his five Academy Award nominations, cementing his international stardom. Additionally, he collected his third (of thirteen) BAFTA nomination, the New York Film Critics Circle Award and two Golden Globe nominations for Best Actor in a Comedy or Musical, and Best Male Newcomer (which he won).

After the huge success of *Tom Jones* and a short spell on the stage, Finney returned to films with Reisz's 1964 drama, *Night Must Fall*, which he also produced. This was followed by Stanley Donen's classic 1967 romantic drama, *Two for the Road*, in which he starred opposite Audrey Hepburn.

Only once during all those years had Finney even mentioned Delaney publicly: on 10th February 1961 on the front page of the *Salford Reporter* he was pictured at home with his family, and in an interview he was asked about her. He replied, "Make no mistake about it, she [Delaney] is important. She is going places. I was most impressed with *Taste of Honey* which I think will become a classic of the new school. I was unfortunately unable to see her second one but I am convinced that she has a great future." He admitted to sharing one eccentricity with her, in that he couldn't stand formal clothing. "I gave my last two [lounge suits] to the refugee collection."[4]

They met at last in late 1965. Finney had brought John Arden's play *Armstrong's Last Goodnight* to the Manchester Opera House while Shelagh was filming *The White Bus* in Salford with Lindsay Anderson. Harold Riley mentioned to him that Shelagh had written an original screenplay and Finney asked to see it. "It was a short document." he said. "More a basic idea than a complete script. But I liked it and found I had a lot of ideas about it, so Shelagh and I decided to work on it together."[5]

The idea that he and Delaney developed had a familiar ring to it: "Shelagh had written about a man of my age returning to my home town. He has had success, but finds it is not important as, well, as other things. No doubt people will read into it more of me than is there by intention. The resemblances are there, but Charlie's dilemma – about success and its meaning or lack of it – is not mine. I think I'm more 'digested' than Charlie."[6]

According to Finney, the two of them discussed the script over the next year, on and off, while Finney worked at the Royal Court and made a film in France. When they finally completed a working script, he decided that he ought to direct it. In 1965, along with fellow actor Michael Medwin, he'd founded a film production company called Memorial Enterprises. He explained: "We didn't want to sit in offices and go in at seven and read scripts and do deals. We felt that now and again we might come across something we'd like to get made or like to see made."[7]

The new script appeared to him worth filming, but "I knew we could only do it my way. I couldn't ask a good director to do it on those terms, so I decided I might as well have a bash myself." *Charlie Bubbles* would thus become Memorial Enterprises' first film.[8]

Although the film would not be autobiographical, it would mean a return to Manchester and Salford, something Delaney had been doing in various creative guises for almost a decade. As we will see, there would appear to have been more of her own life and experience in the story than Finney's.

Throughout the film, Charlie appears largely non-committal and blank-looking, bemused, maybe bored while at the same time watching everyone around him closely. He appears at times as if in a dream out of which he emerges now and then to act. Characters talking to him are often filmed looking directly into the camera, as though the audience is Charlie.

The film opens with Charlie driving a gold-plated Rolls Royce to an exclusive restaurant to meet his financial advisers. He is a successful writer, but his main preoccupation at the dinner is not with tax breaks but with his estranged wife and son living up north whom he is about to visit. He is diverted from the accountants' chatter by an old friend, Smokey (played by Colin Blakely) also having dinner in the restaurant.

Charlie leaves his advisers and joins Smokey. They chat, insult one another good-naturedly and proceed to throw food all over one another in full view of the rest of the exclusive diners. They then walk out still covered in food and find an expensive clothes store where they swap their suits for flat caps and overcoats before embarking on a drinking binge in snooker halls, betting shops and grim, working-class drinking dives.

Charlie is clearly better off than Smokey, who gets far drunker as the evening progresses. They decide to travel north that night and they return to Charlie's house where a series of comic scenes unfold viewed by both Charlie and ourselves through a bank of close-circuit cameras he has had installed in every room. We meet Charlie's assistant Miss Heyhoe (Liza Minnelli in her first film role) and we watch as they eat a meal prepared by grumbling, live-in servants. Finally Charlie, Smokey and Miss Heyhoe leave, but Smokey passes out. They take him home and he is put to bed by his wife. Charlie and Miss Heyhoe then set off for Manchester in the middle of the night where Charlie is expected, having promised to take his son to a football match. (Charlie appears in his wife's eyes as feckless and juvenile: she has already upbraided him on the phone, commenting: "It's time you grew up and faced reality.")

The trip north along the newly constructed M1 is almost a dream-fantasy and of much greater significance back then with 'the North' still appearing to those in 'the South' as being a different land entirely. People whom the couple encounter along the way either watch Charlie sullenly or ignore him. In a deserted motorway service station a glamorous female film star with an entourage joins him and they talk aimlessly. Later, an airman returning home cadges a lift and comments on Charlie's life and what he, the airman, would do with his wealth. Underlying the man's chatter is a sense of jealousy, plus a conviction that, given the breaks, he could have done as well as Charlie. Although he thanks him for the gift of an autographed book, the hiker is less interested in that ("the wife has read all your books") than in an opportunity to drive the car and to empty its cocktail cabinet.

The character Miss Heyhoe, meanwhile, serves as a means of conveying information about where he is returning to and what he has left behind. Although American, she has relatives from Manchester and she is keen to see where they once lived. She mentions the "friendliness of the people", the "regular family correspondence" and the "semi-documentary novel" she wants to write about it all. She also refers to old houses ("Ellis Street") being torn down but with nothing being put back in their place. Charlie appears to have no opinion on this.

They arrive on the outskirts of Manchester and peer down at the city from on high before the Rolls Royce drives around a demolished Salford townscape, Miss Heyhoe snapping pictures all the while. "A shame to pull these lovely old places down, they have so much character," she says. She then comments on Charlie: "A prophet is always without honour in his own country," and almost on cue, a Boys' Brigade band appears and the Rolls follows it across the devastated scene.

They then arrive at the glitzy but provincial splendour of Manchester's Piccadilly Hotel, all muzak and ingratiating staff. The old man serving them breakfast turns out to be an old friend of Charlie's father, which prompts talk of the past and the Depression. "He was unemployed for some years," the man says, and "We're all very proud of you." To his query "Do you just do your writing now, or are you still working?" Bubbles smiles wryly and retorts, "No, I just do the writing," and hands him a banknote as tip.

There follows a semi-catatonic (on Bubbles' part) seduction scene in which Miss Heyhoe undresses him and starts making love. Her hairpiece becomes detached on the pillow and he gazes at it with horror.

The film then shifts gear entirely. The following morning, he travels to his ex-wife Lottie's house in the surrounding hills. He plays with his son while Lottie (played by Billie Whitelaw) potters around the farm, awkwardly collecting eggs, baking bread and complaining that she wished she'd a proper job, that she'd married too soon and that she wouldn't have done these things with hindsight. She seems as stranded as Charlie, though defiantly so.

Father and son Jack then go to the football match where they eat hot dogs in their private box at Manchester United's Old Trafford ground (the first such facility at a football ground in the land). In a long, uneasy scene, Bubbles watches his son watching the game and growing bored and detached. When United score, Jack simply presses his face up against the window as if wishing he could get out there rather than be enclosed in the goldfish bowl.

An old school friend, now a local reporter, arrives in the box and they chatter awkwardly, Bubbles rejecting all overtures to join his friend for a drink or to have his picture taken with his son. The friend declares that he would never leave his 'grass roots', dismissing London and the people down there, who "get bogged down with a lot of false values". There's some animosity between the two men, the friend appearing jealous and resentful. Bubbles then realises he has lost his son and searches for him around the stadium, eventually reporting him to the police but finding himself unable to describe him adequately.

Bubbles returns to the farm without the boy, driving the Rolls erratically and stopping to vomit on the way, only to discover Jack has found his own way home and is now watching television. The last section of the film sees Bubbles and wife arguing over how she is bringing up the boy. She is scornful of his suggestions, while he tries to act the stern father. The boy is clearly spoilt but Bubbles is in no position to do anything about it. There are a couple of comic interventions from intrusive local reporters before Bubbles, exhausted, is put to bed by wife and son.

Next morning, all is deserted, the surrounding hills presenting a sylvan scene. He walks out and across a field and finds a hot air balloon tethered and untended. He climbs in, the balloon soars into the sky and it's the end of the film.

David Slavitt, writing about the film in 2009, considered it to be largely autobiographical: "There is a provincialism, a narrowness, and, yes, an ugliness from which he has been trying to escape, but from which he is now cut off and exiled. These powerfully mixed feelings are what the movie is about, and his discomfort grows to fill the screen and, for the most part, involve the audience. It may not be particularly original, but the sense of the deracination is indisputably authentic. And Finney's investment of himself as director as well as star suggests a special connection with the material."[9]

*Top:* Albert Finney and Liza Minnelli oblige the autograph-hunters in Hankey Park, Salford, October 1967.
*Bottom:* An alluring film poster for an elusive film, 1968.

**Charlie Bubbles.**

As we have seen, when the film was being made, Finney was not so certain about this 'special connection'. "No doubt people will read into it more of me than is there by intention. The resemblances are there, but Charlie's dilemma – about success and its meaning or lack of it – is not mine …"

Finney was correct when he suggested that he was more 'digested' than Charlie Bubbles. In fact, his career path as an actor had followed just the trajectory he'd wanted. Whenever he had grown tired of fame and fortune, he had taken himself off and rested, recharging his batteries until ambition tugged at him once more. Thus, the character he played had very little to do with himself. What's more, Finney plays a writer in the film, not an actor.

Success and its meaning or lack of it would, he explained, be the theme of the film, but the two successful Salfordians, Delaney and himself, would have had different experiences of that success. The hitch-hiker who helps himself to Charlie's drinks and cigars and drives his Rolls Royce says, "I can relate a story, but I can't get it down on paper. I've got the brains, I suppose, but not the education … still, you've done very well out of it …" This is surely Delaney's world rather than Albert Finney's. Delaney has faced such reactions all her life; Finney will not have had to. In *Sweetly Sings the Donkey*, a woman acquaintance Delaney encounters in the street says to her, "Some of us have to work for a living. I'll have to write a play, won't I? Then I can retire as well." (There is something about writing that mystifies people; it seems effortless.)

This thread runs through the film. Journalists, the secretary, strangers or people who knew Charlie in the past all treat him with superficially harmless cliché, deeply rooted, however, in malice towards someone who has made a lot of money at something they feel anyone can do. One imagines that actors are not treated in quite the same way.

Renata Adler felt that "Shelagh Delaney has caught all the insinuating reminders, all the uninvited conversations, all the corrosive nonsense, all the noise that are likely to surround such a man when he is not working, and when he is looking for a little warmth or credible flattery from somewhere."[10]

There was also the question of the returning celebrity: someone from the provinces who has made good and left, possibly for London but who may have found it hard to return and relate to his home town in the same way. Finney had, from the first moment he'd risen to prominence, always received a hero's welcome back in Salford. He was a favourite son, whereas Delaney was very much the black sheep. When interviewed in

2012 about Salford and what it meant to him, he replied that he saw differences when he returned but was quite positive about them. "I accept the fact of change," he said. "The Lowry painting of the industrial north with the factory chimneys and smoke … that was going to be forever. It looked eternal, and yet it's all gone. Now when you see the Test match from Old Trafford on the television, you can actually see the Pennines which you couldn't before. It's change for the better in some ways." He loved to get back to Salford. "It's just part of you. It's in the blood really."[11]

Delaney loved Salford, too, but her work had consistently revealed a deep anxiety about it and its fate. She could not have viewed the disappearance of so much of its social and architectural fabric with the sanguine spirit of Finney. Although not a major thread in the film, the references made by Miss Heyhoe to the disappearing streets, the lost buildings and the vanishing families are all preoccupations of Delaney's.

Most of the criticism of the film centred on the enigmatic nature of Bubbles himself. American Pauline Kael was particularly exercised over Charlie's lack of either emotion or action. At the start of the film she pondered on how passive he was: "hostile servants who could easily be fired, an adoring fan-secretary whom no sensible writer would keep on. Surely these trivia – the servant problems that go with success – can't be what makes Charlie feel empty?" she asks. For her, the character left too many questions unanswered: "Why doesn't Charlie care enough to reach out for anyone or anything? Did he ever feel any different? Has success changed him? Is he a *good* writer? And if so, why is he alienated?"[12]

Ian Christie also commented on the way the film, "avoids diagnosis". The style of the film, blending near-surrealist association with sharp social observation reminded him of *The White Bus* but, as in that film, the central figure remained a blank, undeveloped and unfathomable.[13]

Film critic Stephen Farber agreed, and although he thought the film was funny rather than boring, as some had accused it of being, he felt it was also flimsy because it never explained why Charlie was so bored with his success or why such a man had no alternatives to such a depressing existence. Delaney's script, "superficially lively and psychologically flat", ignored this problem. It effectively illustrated Charlie's malaise, without illuminating it.[14]

Despite this, it was agreed that the final scene, when Charlie and his wife Lottie are sparring and bickering, was where the film really came to life: "How can anyone who really watches these scenes that have the stops and starts of authentic conversation and unspoken affection and frustration, call the movie weary? Perhaps we are too spoiled by flashiness."[15] "Here everything possible has long been said, yet the brief, flat exchanges emerge charged with recollection and irony."[16] Significantly, Whitelaw won the 1968 British Academy of Film and Television Arts award for Best Supporting Actress for her performance.

It is this sequence, perhaps, that explains the film's ultimate failure to connect, to become more than a series of disjointed encounters. The well-written (and acted) final scenes on Lottie's farm dealing with an estranged couple appear to be from a different film entirely, even though they are the culmination of Bubbles' quest. The only motivation for him to act from the very beginning of the film was the promise he had made to take his son to a football match, a promise he'd been reminded of by Lottie, a divorcee caring for her son but isolated and largely powerless. Without that goal, he would have remained in London. His journey north is thus largely irrelevant in narrative terms: he engages with none of the characters along the way, simply watches and endures. When he reaches his goal, he is exhausted and defeated, and ends it all by flying off in a balloon.

Finney's remark that Delaney's story concerned a man who has found "money and success but realises that these are not as important 'as other things ...'" is significant. Much later, in an interview in 1976, when discussing a series of plays she had written for television called *The House That Jack Built*, Delaney talked of the married couple involved as having, "entered into a sacrament. That's the important thing ... It's a divine state, isn't it? That's exactly what I mean. Words are very important and they're not well used these days."

The marriage at the centre of *The House That Jack Built* has survived for ten years, but things are getting difficult. The couple struggle on: "They learn they've got to put up with things they don't really want to put up with ... certain aspects of each other ... they are building something physical and emotional and something collapses and they build it up again." She agreed with the interviewer that the plays "were written as a sort of celebration of marriage".

One senses that Delaney's ultimate preoccupation in the film *Charlie Bubbles* was with a similar topic: a couple's failing/failed marriage. Indeed, this was also at the heart of *Lion in Love*: married couples and their largely irresolvable day-to-day struggles. Charlie Bubbles was clearly in her mind in the interview about *The House That Jack Built* almost a decade later when, in referring to that fact that there was no sex in the plays she continues: "Although the audience expect explicit sex ... it's more potent when it isn't explicit. In *Charlie Bubbles* the first time you see Billie Whitelaw, she's getting out of bed, not getting in, and it's much more sexy."[17]

At the time *Charlie Bubbles* was being made Delaney was herself bringing up her daughter single-handed, just like Lottie. Albert Finney had divorced his first wife just as his career had started to gather speed, leaving her to bring up their child. These factors must have played a part in the shaping of the film, particularly as the 'idea' at the start was a vague one and neither of them were natural film-makers.

The film garnered an award for Shelagh from the Writers' Guild of Great Britain for the Best British Screenplay. However, although released briefly in the United Kingdom in July 1967, it suddenly disappeared, resurfacing at the occasional film festival but missing out on Cannes in 1968 as the festival was cancelled because of student unrest across the continent. It was shown in September 1968 at the Odeon, St Martin's Lane, London which is where John Russell Taylor got to see it, considering it "the most exciting, personal and accomplished feature début by a British director since Lindsay Anderson's *This Sporting Life*". It never went on general release, however.

Albert Finney directed no more films, although his production company would be responsible for a string of classic British movies, involving ironically a couple by Lindsay Anderson, *If ...* and *O Lucky Man!*, the films Anderson said were the result of his experiment with *The White Bus*.

Finney and Delaney remained great friends and planned further films together. In 1981, Finney told Stephen Farber that the two of them had been working on a script "and we had the main thread of the story. But we were confused about the ending. Our hero is with a primitive tribe, and we couldn't decide how to resolve it. One day Shelagh came in and said, 'I've got the ending, Albert. It's perfectly simple. They eat him.' I said, 'Shelagh, in Anglo-Saxon film mythology, you do not eat the hero. It's unheard of for people to go to see a movie where Clint Eastwood or Burt Reynolds will be eaten.' So we've put that script on the shelf. We're waiting until the world comes round to her way of thinking."[18]

NOTES

1  *Guardian*, 23rd September 1989.

2  *Manchester Evening News*, 30th November 2012: 'Actor Albert Finney – Son of Salford – Loves to Come Home'.

3  Ibid.

4  *SCR*, 10th February 1961.

5  *New York Times*, 'Before the Bubble Burst' by Stephen Watts, 27th November 1966.

6  Ibid.

7  Interviewed by Michael Billington at the National Film Theatre on 6 June 1982 (http://www.screenonline.org.uk).

8  *New York Times*, 'Before the Bubble Burst'.

9  David R. Slavitt, 'The Finney Question', *The Hopkins Review*, 2, 2 (Spring 2009).

10  'The Quietly Desperate World of Charlie Bubbles', *New York Times*, 12th February 1968.

11  *Manchester Evening News*, 30th November 2012.

12  Pauline Kael, *Going Steady: Film Writings, 1968-69*, new edn (Marion Boyars, 2004).

13  Ian Christie, *Monthly Film Bulletin*, 35 (1968), p. 148.

14  Stephen Farber in *Film Quarterly*, 21, 4 (Summer, 1968), p. 57.

15  Ibid.

16  Christie in *Monthly Film Bulletin*, 35 (1968).

17  *Guardian*, 4th August 1976.

18  *New York Times*, 26th July 1981: 'Finney Comes Back to Film', by Stephen Farber.

# 18

# Epilogue

Delaney still retains a directness, and a simplicity in conversation (once she decides to speak) which she brought from the North, though now other places beckon.

*The Guardian*, August 1976

When Shelagh Delaney died in 2011, the majority of obituaries suggested that, with the failure of *Lion In Love*, she had ceased to be a writer of any significance. Even Jeanette Winterson, who called Delaney her 'hero' considered that after *Honey* Shelagh had quietly petered out. The reason, according to Winterson, was that she had been badly let down by the literary establishment. "She had the talent and we let her go." When her second play failed, 'Nobody turned things around for Delaney."[1]

To suggest that Shelagh Delaney was not given support and simply faded away does her and those she subsequently worked with a great disservice. Though she suffered at the hands of bigots – her treatment by her home town or those in a position to consider themselves the official spokespersons for Salford was a scandal, bordering at times on the libellous – she was not a hapless victim. One has to consider the individual rather than the stereotype.

Her first two plays were certainly heavily criticised, principally by male critics, whose perspectives were often skewed by Delaney's age and gender. Such was the nature of the times. But as we have seen, Delaney had many significant champions during this period. John Osborne, Wolf Mankowitz and Oscar Lewenstein backed her, and *Lion in Love* was given not one chance but two. It might have been left to die in the provinces but was brought to the Royal Court, while few playwrights get the chance, as Delaney did, of an off-Broadway production. One might say that no one succeeded in turning her playwriting career around, but it can't be said that no one tried. What's more, she appears to have left Theatre Workshop in wilful fashion, refusing to take Joan Littlewood's advice because the fabled director would not indulge her. (Though they fell out briefly, they were soon reconciled to the point where Joan Littleowood even asked Delaney to take over Theatre Workshop some years later.)

With her long-promised third play failing to appear, Lewenstein, who had taken an option on her subsequent work, then backed her prose stories and recruited top young film directors such as Tony Richardson, Karel Reitz and Lindsay Anderson to develop them into films in close conjunction with Delaney. Immediately after that, Albert Finney's Memorial Enterprises film company developed another of her ideas for his first feature film. During this period, she could be said to have been at the very heart of artistic Britain.

The abrupt break with Theatre Workshop in 1959 revealed a young writer with decided views on her own worth, and it wouldn't be the last time that she demanded full-on attention. In 1970 she worked with director Bryan Forbes on a feature film called *The Raging Moon*, but they fell out and she insisted on her name being taken off the credits. She explained: "Bryan Forbes told me that I'd been spoilt by directors. I had, but there was no reason why I shouldn't have been. Every director I have worked with has taken me giant strides forward."[2]

Where the production of work was concerned, she admitted more than once that she was not prolific. "I tend to be lazy and only work when I have the sort of challenge which is presented by a successful first play," she said soon after *A Taste of Honey* appeared. Of the long silences in her output she admitted in 1976: "I've got a very slow one-track mind. It takes me years to think. But I write very quickly. I need a deadline. One half of me is a perfectionist; the other is a lazy good-for-nothing." In this same interview, she revealed that she was about to go to America to write a commissioned novel. Her aim was to write it in six weeks. "But I don't know if I'll be seduced by the fleshpots of Cape Cod away from my Parker pen." The novel did not appear.[3]

In fact, a pattern was established during the immediate post-*Honey* years, that of a gifted writer who worked well in collaboration with others and whose niche would ultimately be writing scripts for films and later television, where her skill at dialogue and characterisation could be fully developed, where her desire to capture character in motion rather than in developing rounded stories could be realised. None of this suggests a writer fading and given the opportunities regularly afforded her, certainly not one being abandoned or disregarded.

If anything, it was the other way round: Delaney appears to have decided that after the maelstrom of activity that engulfed her following the success of *Honey* public appearances, the life of the celebrity writer was not for her. Thus, only once between the announcement of her baby's birth in 1964 and early 2000 did she grant newspapers or television any significant opportunity to hear or see her. In 1976 she consented to give the *Guardian* a short interview as a prelude to the six-part television series, *The House That Jack Built*. The BBC, incidentally, had given her a free hand to write anything she chose. She was by now settled in Islington, North London, where her daughter was about to enter Islington Green secondary school. She hadn't been inactive since her work on *Charlie Bubbles*: in the same year as *Raging Moon*, in 1970, she had produced her first original television play, *Did Your Nanny Come from Bergen?*, one of the acclaimed BBC TV Thirty-Minute Theatre series. This had been followed in 1974 by another television play, *St Martin's Summer*, part of an omnibus production for ITV called *The Seven Faces of Woman*, examining 'various aspects of contemporary woman at seven different ages'. Delaney's story concerned a divorced woman in her fifties who goes into hospital where she meets a young male patient who enables her to look at her other relationships in a new light. With theme music provided by the French singer Charles Aznavour and further plays by talented writers including Andrea Newman and Jack Rosenthal, *Seven Faces* an was extremely popular series.

*The House That Jack Built* (1976) was considered a return, of sorts, after years of being out of the publicity limelight. Delaney revealed to Kenneth Saunders: "I wrote *The House That Jack Built* as a stage play. It could easily have been done on the stage. Joan (Littlewood) liked them so much she would have liked to have done them."[4]

Delaney described the series as being about ten years in the married life of Jack and Lu ("a cowboy and a Madonna", as she dubbed them) from their wedding night to the present time. Jack is an engineer, Lu used to be a shorthand typist. The storyline dealt with Delaney's perpetual preoccupations: the necessity to endure family life and its inevitable problems with humour, rather than seeking too hard to find elusive solutions. Reality, she warns, will always prick the bubble of romance. In fact, she would appear to have plucked Frank and Nora from out of *Lion in Love* and turned them into Jack and Lu. Just as in *Lion in Love*, where Frank has a dream of leaving his wife and setting up a small shop elsewhere, Frank has a dream of buying a castle in Scotland, their present house being due for demolition.

Jack's yearnings, like Frank's, are shown up as pure fantasy. When Lu begins to take him seriously he finds all sorts of objections to going on with the scheme – as Lu says, "For all your extravagant talk you're just as stuck in the mud as everybody else." Lu, by contrast, says, "I admit my visions are a bit thin on the ground, but when something does take my fancy I like to see it develop." This could be Nora speaking.

In the end they move into a house situated in kind of no-man's land, neither town nor country, not even a proper suburb. It's somewhere adjacent to a motorway, within sight of a field. Saddled with an enormous mortgage, their lives now dominated by money worries, their banter loses its sparkle. Jack worries about growing old and jokes grimly about pensioners, while Lu begins to suspect that he's going to leave her for someone younger. Instead, after she finds a job and regains her self-respect, it's she who walks out on him. While they're apart, they think of nothing but each other, and this yearning for one another finally overcomes even Lu's dread of a return to the prison-house of marriage. The play series was well received critically and would be adapted for the stage in America a couple of years later.

Over the next thirty years, Delaney would build a solid body of work, mining many of the themes she had established in her early years. There would be more prose stories, plus television plays and film scripts including 1985's *Dance with a Stranger*, the story of the hanged murderess Ruth Ellis which would win the Prix Populaire at the Cannes Film Festival.

Meanwhile, *A Taste of Honey* would continue to be produced in theatres in Britain and around the world. It was adapted for British television in the early 1970s, starring Diana Dors and Barry Foster, and was filmed twice more: in 1981 for Spanish TV and in 1994 for a Portuguese production company. The play text itself (as well as *Sweetly Sings the Donkey*) has also featured on GCSE schools curricula since the 1980s, introducing her work to generation after generation of young readers. On stage hardly a year passes without a revival somewhere. In 1982 the New York Century Theatre production ran for almost a year and earned Amanda Plummer various awards on her Broadway début.

Fifty years on from its first appearance, a special programme on BBC was devoted to examining both the play and film. As the novelist and critic D.J. Taylor judged, "For all the interpretative zeal expended during last week's anniversary tribute [*A Taste of Honey*] began to look as much like a sociological artefact as a piece of dramatic art."[5]

Delaney would, inevitably, given her gender, be regularly referenced in the developing world of sexual politics. Colette Lindroth suggested: "Feminists especially should find her rebellious, sexually independent female characters intriguing. Tough, unsentimental, often unlucky but always resilient, their insistence on aggressive self-definition came well before that stance became fashionable."[6]

Increasingly, those assessing this landmark play from an evolving feminist angle have discovered aspects of it that challenge and re-evaluate social roles and assumptions. Michelene Wandor suggested: "The issues and dilemmas are radical: motherhood is thrust on many women; nurturing is not necessarily an automatic maternal instinct, whereas a man may well feel 'maternal', yet be prevented from being able to express himself."[7] Jozefina Komporaly agreed: "The realization that female destiny is thrust upon her [Jo] triggers her deepest fears, conveyed most convincingly when she talks about breastfeeding: 'I'm not having a little animal nibbling away at me, it's cannibalistic. Like being eaten alive.'"[8]

Some have suggested Delaney was a proto-feminist merely in representing such lives and celebrating the strength of such women on stage. However, her decision to bring mother and daughter back together again at the end of the play to take on the burden of childbirth suggested "a maintenance of traditional roles: Helen returns to her pregnant daughter and Geoffrey has to leave. In this respect, Delaney does not succeed in challenging the dominant ideology of her time."[9]

But as to the play itself, that question remains: Sociological artefact or dramatic art? Does it still have any resonance with modern audiences or is it now simply a time-capsule, redolent of an era long since passed away?

The half-centenary of its début in 2008 saw the play revived with a star cast in Manchester's Royal Exchange. Helen was played by Sally Lindsay, who brought with her a shared audience memory of her role as the barmaid Shelley in *Coronation Street*, a character who might almost have been in *A Taste of Honey*. Lindsay declared: "I'm extremely proud more than anything, because obviously I'm a Mancunian actress, and this is my hometown and who I am …"[10]

Could *A Taste of Honey* still shock people as it had back in 1958? There was a general consensus among theatre critics that of course it couldn't, but that what had always been its key ingredient – the essential quality of Delaney's writing – still gripped.

"Some of Delaney's themes may feel dated but her writing still glitters dangerously and wittily," the late Lynne Walker of the *Independent* wrote. "*A Taste of Honey* remains a passionate statement about real people trapped in poverty, deprived of ambition and vulnerable to manipulation by the fickleness of others."[11]

Sam Marlowe for *The Times* thought: "Brawling, boozing, teenage pregnancy and fractured families: Shelagh Delaney's benchmark drama ... has lost none of its relevance 50 years on ... The quirkiness and passion of Delaney's young voice still rings out ... It remains passionate and pungent."[12] *The Guardian*'s Michael Billington concluded, "Delaney's achievement was to write, with comic vividness, about the world she knew ... the tone is often raucously comic, and the final message is of the human spirit's capacity for survival."[13]

The play's director Jo Combes was adamant that it retained contemporary significance: Jo remained a truly desperate character at the end, despite what Combes saw as Delaney's "absence of complete despair". Jo has given birth and has nowhere to go. "This is Shelagh Delaney highlighting the lack of opportunities in life for girls like Jo, their lives utterly changed at a young age. It was something that she obviously felt passionate about."[14]

One aspect of Combes' production that failed to please all, however, was the replacement on stage of the original jazz band in Joan Littlewood's London production. Instead, the Exchange production had a DJ playing a live mix of classic tunes from various 1980s Manchester-based pop groups such as The Stone Roses, The Bees, Inspiral Carpets and Joy Division ('Love Will Tear Us Apart'). This reflected an aspect of Delaney's influence that had gone well beyond the stage.

In the 1980s numerous lines from *A Taste of Honey* and *Lion in Love* had been liberally plundered by Manchester pop star Morrissey and the Smiths, who also put her face on one of their best-selling records. Morrissy claimed that "at least fifty per cent of my reason for writing can be blamed on Shelagh Delaney." He later admitted, "I know I overdid it with Shelagh Delaney. It took me a long, long time to shed that particular one."[15]

The decision to include the more contemporary music was a deliberate attempt by Combes to stick close to what she saw as Joan Littlewood's vision of the play rather than that of Richardson's film. "This is all part of the way I see the play as something fresh and exciting and not a museum piece. There is a restless energy at work that fascinates me. Much in the play also seems dream-like and I shall be suggesting this."[16]

The *Guardian* reviewer liked the innovation: "Jo Combes's revival not only looks like a Smiths album sprung to life, it comes packaged with appropriate songs, which has a historically disorientating effect but seems in keeping with the play's joyfully unconventional spirit."[17]

Sam Marlowe was less convinced: "Unfortunately, the anachronistic choice of music detracts from the Fifties setting, particularly when the actors break into full-blown choreographed routines that, rather than enhance the action, impede its flow and intensity – deeply problematic, given that the play is meandering and tonally confused."[18]

Lynne Walker agreed. 'The music certainly brings the production up to date but the play remains firmly rooted in the 1950s. The interaction between stage and DJ – like the interaction between the actors and the audience – is a conceptual polish that, instead of adding a finish, gets in the way of theatrical interest."[19]

Which suggested that, despite the passage of time, productions of *A Taste of Honey* could still cause controversy. However, its success in 2008 and its hearty welcome in the urban hinterland that had spawned it underlined one particular truth about the play. Jo Combes had said before the opening: "This play seems to belong to the people of Salford. Whenever I tell anyone from Salford I'm involved with this, they claim ownership. No one despairs in this play as far as I'm concerned and it's this positive side of the play that I'll be concentrating on. I'm after the 'Salford swagger' if you like, an attitude of mind that's unique to that area."[20]

The decade from 1958, when *A Taste of Honey* first appeared on stage, and 1968, when *Charlie Bubbles* made its belated appearance, had seen Delaney return again and again to the city of her birth, either as an indirect version of herself (Jo), a surrogate self (the Girl in the *White Bus*), or as her real-life self (in Ken Russell's *Monitor* film). She had roamed the market-place in *Lion in Love*, and recreated her childhood and adolescence in *Sweetly Sings the Donkey*. She had even tried to build her own permanent workplace there with the attempt to create a community theatre.

It's no wonder, therefore, that Salford- and Manchester-based artists and writers have, ever since then, claimed her as a creative inspiration and a literary pathfinder. For some it even seemed that *A Taste of Honey* was a foreshadowing of practically every northern working-class drama showcase from *Coronation Street* to *The Royle Family*. ("Without *A Taste of Honey* there would be no *Coronation Street*," Combes said confidently. "If you look at those early, grim black-and-white episodes of that programme, you can see almost a mirror image of the play.")[21]

In 2003 Comma Press, an independent publishing house based in Manchester's Northern Quarter was founded by Ra Page and is still a prolific publisher of short fiction in the UK today. To mark its launch, a collection of specially commissioned, urban short stories was published, including a new story from Delaney called 'Abduction'. Other contributors included young northern dramatists, novelists and journalists only a couple of whom had even been born when Delaney's *Taste of Honey* arrived in the West End. It might be argued that none of them could have existed in the same way without Shelagh Delaney.

Jeanette Winterson was in no doubt, writing in 2010: "Delaney was born in Salford in 1938. I was born in Manchester in 1959. Same background, same early success. She was like a lighthouse – pointing the way and warning about the rocks underneath. She was the first working-class woman playwright."[22]

In the last decade of her life, Delaney produced a series of radio scripts. A new version of *A Taste of Honey*, inevitably, would feature among them but there would also be new plays including a three-part reworking and development of her prose piece, 'Sweetly Sings the Donkey'. These three stories (the second two being called 'Tell Me a Film' and 'Baloney Said Salome') completed her working life-cycle.

In them, she takes her semi-fictional self along with three of her childhood friends on a journey from post-Second World War innocence right up to desperate old age. In the last story, she ruminates on her cinema-going days, on her carefree life in 1960s Paris, on the necessity of old friends sticking together until the very end. She also reflects on the destruction of her home town where there is hardly anything left of what used to be, where the roads are lined with warehouses and unwanted flats, where a shabby shopping centre stands in place of a once vibrant market – a city that "has had its heart pulled out".

By coincidence, or perhaps not, at about the time she was writing the scripts in July 2001, Shelagh stepped out of the shadows and returned to Salford to join a project/campaign to save the Ambassador Cinema from demolition. Opened in 1928 as one of the area's first 'Super Cinemas' and the last such ancient venue surviving in Salford, the Ambassador was a well-preserved building boasting a marble staircase with metal balustrade on fluted posts, decorative coloured glass windows, an auditorium with a coffered ceiling and fluted Art Deco-style mouldings. It also housed an organ made by the famous Old Trafford firm Jardine & Co. specifically for the cinema to accompany silent films. Its resident pianist for many years had been Violet Carson, better known as Ena Sharples of *Coronation Street*.

Shelagh, described by her local paper as the 'reclusive playwright who shuns the limelight', told the *Salford Star*: "It was built when people went to the pictures at least twice a week. My family were no exception. Salford has preserved few of its historic buildings. It cannot afford to lose the Ambassador. Joining the Ambassador project is more than just a desire to pay respect to the past. The project will not treat the building as a museum piece. It will have to earn its living once again as a cinema, and also as a theatre, restaurant and meeting place where people can have a good time. Saving the Ambassador will not only preserve something good from Salford's past, it will add something good to the life of Salford present."[23]

The campaign had echoes of the 1961 Community Theatre project. Now, as then, it was all in vain. Salford City Council showed, at best indifference and at worst open hostility to the idea of saving what was at the time a Grade II listed building. The Ambassador was subsequently de-listed and a year later planning bosses agreed to demolish the 74-year-old building in favour of two apartment blocks containing thirty-one flats. Two years later, it was finally flattened.

It was as if the Salford Council of Shelagh Delaney's past had risen one last time to deliver a final slap in the face to an artist whom they had never understood and one whom they had certainly never deserved.

NOTES
1   Jeanette Winterson, *The Guardian*, Saturday 18th September 2010.
2   *Guardian*, 4th August 1976.
3   Ibid.
4   Ibid.
5   D.J. Taylor in *The Tablet*, 31st May 2008.
6   Colette Lindroth, 'Shelagh Delaney', in William W. Demastes (ed.), *British Playwrights, 1956–1995: A Research and Production Sourcebook* (Westport, CT: Greenwood, 1996), pp. 119–28.
7   Michelene Wandor in *Post-war British Drama: Looking Back in Gender* (Routledge, 2001).
8   Jozefina Komporaly, *Staging Motherhood: British Women Playwrights, 1956 to the Present* (Palgrave Macmillan, 2006).
9   Eva Meissenpichler 'British Women Dramatists in the Second Half of the Twentieth Century: The Role of Mothers' (Master's degree thesis, University of Vienna, 2009).
10  Sally Lindsay in *Metro* (Manchester), 11th November 2008.
11  *Independent Extra*, 19th November 2008: 'Music Fails to Enhance this Grim Slice of Life; TASTE OF HONEY, Royal Exchange Theatre, Manchester'.
12  *The Times*, 19th November 2008: 'A Rough Tale Passionately Told' by Sam Marlowe.
13  Michael Billington, *Guardian*, 19th November 2008.
14  'A Taste of Honey: Philip Hamer Celebrates the Fiftieth Anniversary of Shelagh Delaney's Salford Classic – and Talks to the Director of its Forthcoming Royal Exchange Revival', 12th November 2008. http://www.manchesterconfidential.co.uk/
15  Andrew Male in *Mojo* (April 2006).
16  Philip Hamer (see no. 14).
17  Alfred Hickling, *Guardian*, 20th November 2008.
18  *The Times*, 19th November 2008.

19   *Independent Extra*, 19th November 2008.
20   See no. 14.
21   Ibid.
22   Jeanette Winterson, *Guardian*, 18th September 2010.
23   'Playwright Joins Historic Cinema Fight', *Salford Star*, 11th July 2001.

# Appendix

# Shelagh Delaney in Pictures

In the early years of her writing career, Shelagh Delaney's gender was clearly an issue with many male reviewers and commentators. Their blatantly sexist treatment of both her and her work was remarkable, even for the time. However, for every cloud there is a silver lining and possibly no other female writer before the advent of the modern celebrity culture has found herself the object of such close photographic attention. Between 1958 and 1962 she was the subject of some of the most eminent photographers in the world, all of them drawn to her striking looks, not to mention her unconventional manner. Quite simply, the camera loved her.

As early as 1958, the avant-garde photographer Ida Kar took a series of portraits of Shelagh, close-up high-contrast black-and-white prints that took their place among other similar portraits in a ground-breaking exhibition of Kar's work at the Whitechapel Gallery in 1960. Kar was the first photographer to have a retrospective exhibition at a major London art gallery. Mounted onto blocked board and sold as one-offs, each portrait bore comparison with a painting. Others of her subjects included the artists Henry Moore, Georges Braque, Gino Severini and Bridget Riley as well as writers such as Iris Murdoch and Jean-Paul Sartre.

In 1959, Shelagh was snapped by Dan Farson, the TV presenter, whose excellent photographic work of the period is now featured in galleries around the world, including the National Portrait Gallery.

In 1959 and 1960, top *Vogue* fashion photographers Norman Parkinson and Brian Duffy took contrasting pictures of her, Duffy taking her outside and into the streets in a manner similar to his work with the top sixties models of the day.

In 1961, as we have seen, American Arnold Newman, often credited with being the first photographer to use so-called environmental portraiture, in which the photographer places the subject in a carefully controlled setting to encapsulate the essence of the individual's life and work, took a series of pictures of Shelagh posing against key Salford scenes – photos that summed up to perfection her personality and contemporary significance.

A year earlier, in Paris, the freelance American Jack Nisberg, who specialised in snapping famous artists, intellectuals, cuisine chefs, politicians and socialites of the time, followed her for the *Observer* as she roamed the boulevards selecting clothes. Nisberg, who worked mainly for *Look*, *Newsweek*, the *Observer*, the *New York Times*, the *Sunday Times*, *Elle Magazine* and *Vogue*, owned one of the largest private collections of prints by contemporary photographers in the world, and his work is now housed in the world-famous Roger-Viollet collection in Paris.

Back in London in 1962, Madame Yevonde (Yevonde Cumbers Middleton), doyenne of English society portrait photographers, who pioneered the use of colour in portrait photography, caught Shelagh in a series of contemplative poses. Appropriately, Yevonde, who'd been a suffragette in her teens, used her work to explore issues of gender and identity and many aspects of women's social and sexual roles.

These and many more photographers of significance found Shelagh a fascinating subject, making her one of the most sensitively photographed and recognisable personalities on the London scene until she decided to take herself off into semi-seclusion after 1964.

Dan Farson's photo of Shelagh Delaney outside her Duchy Road home in early 1959.

# Further Reading

For those wishing to follow up issues and themes of the period covered in this book, the following titles are the most important.

## Books

Aldgate, Anthony, *Censorship and the Permissive Society: British Cinema and Theatre 1955–1965* (Clarendon Press, 1995)

Anderson, Lindsay (ed. Paul Sutton), *The Diaries (Diaries, Letters and Essays)* (Methuen Drama, 2006)

Berney, K.A. and N.G. Templeton (eds.), *Contemporary British Dramatists* (St James Press, 1994)

Demastes, William W. (ed.), *British Playwrights, 1956–1995: A Research and Production Sourcebook* (Greenwood, 1996)

Goorney, Howard, *The Theatre Workshop Story* (Methuen, 2008)

Goorney, Howard and Ewan MacColl, *Agit-prop to Theatre Workshop* (Manchester University Press, 1986)

Gourdin-Sangouard, Isabelle, Kathryn Hannan, John Izod and Karl Mage, *Lindsay Anderson: Cinema Authorship* (Manchester University Press, 2012)

Higson, Andrew (ed.), *Dissolving Views: Key Writings on British Cinema* (Continuum International, 1996)

Holdsworth, Nadine, *Joan Littlewood* (Routledge, 2006)

Holdsworth, Nadine, *Joan Littlewood's Theatre* (Cambridge University Press, 2011)

Lacey, Stephen, *British Realist Theatre: The New Wave in Its Context 1956–1965.* (Routledge, 1995)

Littlewood Joan, *Joan's Book: Joan Littlewood's Peculiar History as She Tells It* (Methuen Drama, 2003)

Marowitz Charles, Tom Milne and Owen Hale (eds.), *The 'Encore' Reader: A Chronicle of the New Drama* (Methuen, 1965)

Page, Adrian, *The Death of the Playwright? Modern British Drama and Literary Theory* (Palgrave Macmillan, 1992)

Peacock, D. Keith, *Changing Performance: Culture and Performance in the British Theatre since 1945*, Stage and Screen Studies Series, 11 (Peter Lang, 2007)

Rebellato, Dan, *1956 and All That: The Making of Modern British Drama* (Routledge, 1999)

Taylor, John Russell, *Anger and After: A Guide to the New British Drama* (Pelican Books, 1963)

Wandor, Michelene, *Post-war British Drama: Looking Back in Gender* (Routledge, 2001)

Zarhy-Levo, Yael, *The Making of Theatrical Reputations: Studies from the Modern London Theatre* (University of Iowa Press 2008)

### Articles

Harker, Ben, 'Missing Dates: Theatre Workshop in History', *History Workshop Journal*, 66, 1 (2008), pp. 272–9

Higson, Andrew, 'Space, Place, Spectacle, Landscape and Townscape in the "Kitchen Sink" film', *Screen* 25, 4–5 (July–October 1984)

Meissenpichler, Eva, 'British Women Dramatists in the Second Half of the Twentieth Century: The Role of Mothers' (Master's degree thesis, University of Vienna, 2009)

Patton, Alec, 'Jazz and Music-Hall Transgressions in Theatre Workshop's Production of *A Taste of Honey*', *New Theatre Quarterly*, 23, 4 (November 2007)

Waters, Chris. 'Representations of Everyday Life: L. S. Lowry and the Landscape of Memory in Postwar Britain', *Representations*, 65 (1999)

# Index

# OTHER GREENWICH EXCHANGE TITLES
# BY JOHN HARDING

## A BEND IN THE RIVER: V.S. NAIPAUL

£7.99 (pbk)
ISBN: 978-1-906075-74-3  58pp
Focus On Series

V.S. Naipaul's *A Bend in the River* has long been one of the most
controversial novels written about contemporary Africa. Though based
on Mobutu Sese Seko's rule of the Democratic Republic of the Congo
during the 1970s, it tackles issues that still bedevil the continent today and
is often cited by Naipaul's critics and detractors as evidence of his
inherent pessimism concerning the future of Africa and indeed much of
the post-colonial 'Third World'. This Focus book considers some of those
criticisms of the novel and assesses their validity.

## DREAMING OF BABYLON
## The Life and Times of Ralph Hodgson

£9.99 (pbk)
ISBN: 978-1-906075-00-2  238pp
Biography

Ralph Hodgson was already a brilliant graphic artist and innovator in the
field of Victorian children's comics when, in the early 1900s, he began
producing poetry imbued with a spiritual passion for the beauty of
creation and the mystery of existence. Admired by T.S. Eliot, John
Berryman, Stephen Spender and e.e. cummings, his work has continued
to draw praise from more contemporary writers such as Robert Nye,
Martin Seymour-Smith and Studs Terkel.

In writing this first-ever biography on Hodgson, John Harding has been
able to draw on a wealth of previously unseen material from both sides of
the Atlantic. In doing so he has brought to life one of England's most
intriguing and significant literary characters. Illustrated with Hodgson's
original cartoons and line-drawings, *Dreaming of Babylon* is sure to
capture yet another generation of readers for Hodgson's timeless verse.

# PATRICK HAMILTON

£9.99 (pbk)
ISBN: 978-1-871551-99-0  116pp
Series: Student Guide

Patrick Hamilton was one of the most gifted and admired writers of his generation. Born in Sussex in 1904, he published his first novel, *Craven House* in 1926 and within a few years had established a wide readership for himself. Despite personal setbacks and an increasing problem with drink, he went on to produce some of the most penetrating and influential fiction of the mid-20th century.

John Harding provides a critical appraisal of all of Hamilton's major novels, as well as his successful stage plays, *Rope* and *Gaslight*. He draws on views of a wide variety of commentators, including Michael Holroyd, Doris Lessing, Claud Cockburn and many others, as well as considering how Hamilton's political beliefs affected his work. The book will appeal to both students of English Literature as well as the general reader.

# THE LAST BLACKBIRD & OTHER POEMS
# Ralph Hodgson

## edited by John Harding

£7.95 (pbk)
978-1-871551-81-5  68pp
Poetry

Ralph Hodgson (1871-1962) was a poet and illustrator whose most influential and enduring work appeared to great acclaim just prior to, and during, the First World War.

Though never fashionable, his status among poets down the years has grown. Admired by Eliot, Berryman, Spender and e.e. cummings, his work continues to draw praise from contemporary writers.

This new selection brings together, for the first time in 40 years, some of the most beautiful and powerful 'hymns to life' in the English language.

# SELECTED TITLES

## from GREENWICH EXCHANGE

## ANTONIN ARTAUD

### Lee Jamieson

£9.99 (pbk)
ISBN: 978-1-871551-98-3 108pp
Series: Student Guide

Antonin Artaud's ideas and the terms invented by him – most famously the 'Theatre of Cruelty' – are a vital part of contemporary theatre's everyday vocabulary.

This book demonstrates how his theories, his practice and his influence interlink by exploring Artaud's proposal for a Theatre of Cruelty and assessing the extent to which he achieved his aims during his own lifetime. The final chapter employs practical workshops to demonstrate how Artuad's ideas have manifested themselves in contemporary performance.

Lee Jamieson lectured in drama and theatre studies for over five years at Stratford-upon-Avon College. He currently works in Cyprus as a freelance writer and journalist. He has also written a book on Harold Pinter as part of the Greenwich Exchange Focus On series.

## A. E. HOUSMAN

### Spoken and Unspoken Love

### Henry Maas

£7.99 (pbk)
ISBN: 978-1-906075-73-6 62pp
Literature

*A Shropshire Lad* by A.E. Housman is one of the best-loved books of poems in English, but even now its author remains a shadowy figure. He maintained an iron reserve about himself – and with good reason. His emotional life was dominated by an unrequited love for an Oxford friend.

*Spoken and Unspoken Love* discusses Housman's poetry, especially the effect of an existence deprived of love, as seen in the posthumous work, where the story becomes clear in personal and deeply moving poems.

Henry Maas is an editor and specialist in late nineteenth-century English art and literature, particularly in the work of Oscar Wilde, Aubrey Beardsley, Ernest Dowson and A. E. Housman. His *Ernest Dowson: Poetry and Love in the 1890s* was published by Greenwich Exchange in 2009.

## JOHN KEATS
## Against All Doubtings
## Andrew Keanie

£10.99 (pbk)
ISBN: 978-1-906075-75-0  110pp
Literature

Having identified him as a sort of semi-educated little cockney chancer, Keats's contemporary reviewers savaged him in the pages of Britain's most influential magazines. High ambition, unaccompanied by high birth, and radical affiliations and liberal inclinations, made him an object of contempt to those of, or aping the opinions of, the literary Establishment. In the short term, he never stood a chance.

Long after his death, his reputation was eventually brightened by much more enthusiastic – if, as some have since argued, misguided – appreciations for his beautiful and powerful otherworldliness.

This largely text-focused study promotes the best energies of a more Romantic view of a key Romantic figure.

Andrew Keanie is a lecturer at the University of Ulster. He is the author of student guides to Wordsworth, S.T. Coleridge, Byron and Shelley, a book on Wordsworth and Coleridge, and the first full-length study of Hartley Coleridge since 1931. He lives in Derry with his wife and daughter.

# LAUGHTER IN THE DARK
## The Plays of Joe Orton
### Arthur Burke

£9.99 (pbk)
ISBN: 978-1-871551-56-3  100pp
Series: Student Guide

Arthur Burke examines the two facets of Joe Orton. Orton the playwright had a rare ability to delight and shock audiences with such outrageous farces as *Loot* and *What the Butler Saw*. Orton the man was a promiscuous homosexual caught up in a destructive relationship with a jealous and violent older man. In this study – often as irreverent as the plays themselves – Burke dissects Orton's comedy and traces the connection between the lifestyle and the work.

A former TV critic and comedian, Arthur Burke is a writer and journalist.

# SECOND WORLD WAR POETRY
# IN ENGLISH
## John Lucas

£14.99 (pbk)
ISBN: 978-1-906075-78-1  236pp
Literature

John Lucas's new book sets out to challenge the widely-held assumption that the poetry of the Second World War is, at best, a poor relation to that produced by its predecessor. He argues that the best poetry that came out of the 1939-45 war, while very different from the work of Owen, Rosenberg, Gurney, and their contemporaries, is in no sense inferior.

John Lucas is a poet, novelist, critic and literary historian. His work includes *England and Englishness: Poetry and National Identity, 1688-1914*, *Modern English Poetry: Hardy to Hughes*, and *Starting to Explain: Twentieth-Century British and Irish Poetry*. He is Professor Emeritus at the Universities of Loughborough and Nottingham Trent.

# PAPERS
## Hollie McNish

£11.95 (pbk)
978-1-906075-67-5  76pp
Poetry

Hollie McNish's poetry moves with the rhythms, the excitements and disappointments of contemporary life.

Writing more often than not in the intensity of the moment, McNish views our world aslant to produce sometimes startling, sometimes uncomfortable truths.

*Papers* gathers together the best of McNish's work to date.

for information on these and other great Greenwich Exchange books, visit our website: www.greenex.co.uk